Regina Cœli

by

Fr. Michael Morris, O.P.

Publisher: Pierre-Marie Dumont
Editor: Romain Lizé
Iconography: Isabelle Mascaras
Layout: Elena Germain
Production: Thierry Dubus, Sabine Marioni
Proofreader: Claire Gilligan

ISBN: 978-1-941709-33-7

First edition: September 2016
Printed by Marquis, Canada
Photo engraving: Les Caméléons, Paris

Regina Cœli

*Art and Essays
on the Blessed Virgin Mary*

Fr. Michael Morris, O.P.

MAGNIFICAT®

Paris · New York · Oxford · Madrid

FOREWORD

By Father Peter John Cameron, O.P.

I BELIEVE FATHER MICHAEL MORRIS meant this book on the Blessed Mother to be his masterpiece. But I don't think he ever imagined it would be his last book. Neither did I.

Father Michael Thomas Morris, O.P., died on July 15, 2016.

You will see from reading these exquisite essays that Father Morris subscribed to a conviction held by the renowned English author J.R.R. Tolkien: "All my own perception of beauty, both in majesty and simplicity, is founded upon our Lady."

Father Morris and I had been the best of friends since 1990, when I was assigned to an apostolate in Los Angeles, California—the state where he was born and where he lived. Since the inception of MAGNIFICAT in 1998, Father Morris played an instrumental role in making that publication a monumental success. His superb monthly art commentaries were the hands-down favorite of countless readers. The Blessed Virgin Mary was the subject of dozens of those commentaries.

The plans to publish this book became finalized in the spring of 2016. And then, in May of that year, Father Morris learned he was ill with stage IV cancer. Rather than deter his resolve, the diagnosis only spurred him on to write the best, most beautiful book on the Mother of God that circumstances would allow him. What started out as a heartfelt, personal tribute to the glorious Queen of Heaven turned out instead to be a great, last love letter.

What is more, Mary helped him write it. The night before Father Morris' funeral, at a vigil prayer service packed with admirers, his friend of many years, Dominican Father Michael Carey, delivered a moving eulogy. In his remarks he said:

> Toward the end of his life, Michael intensified his devotion to the Blessed Virgin. To Father Michael, Mary was a gloriously beautiful living icon of God among us. When I visited Michael in May, just shortly after his diagnosis, we spent hours together speaking of the more important things. When he wasn't feeling well, he would lie in bed, and I'd sit beside him, and we'd talk. After one longer conversation, I suggested that we say a rosary together, and he said, "Yes. Let's do that. It will be my third rosary today." He didn't sleep well, and when he woke at night, he said he would pray what he called his midnight rosary.

In the afternoon of July 15th, Father Morris was returning from the hospital where he had gone that morning to receive a medical treatment. I accompanied him to the front door of the rectory, and he expressed how much better he felt and that he was filled with energy. But upon taking the first steps into the corridor leading to his bedroom, he suddenly became short of breath. Just as I rushed behind him, he collapsed to the floor.

I called 911. The dispatcher talked me through CPR. As I administered it to Father Morris, the dispatcher told me to count out loud, and that she would count along with me. But I could not help myself from praying, *Hail Mary, full of grace.... Holy Mary, Mother of God, pray for us sinners, now and at the hour of our death.* And I know the Blessed Virgin honored that begging.

Father Morris never revived.

The priest who helped us penetrate the beauty of art and to delight in its mysteries had a special fondness for an alternative version of the Hail Mary approved in 1847 by Pope Pius IX. It is my belief that this was the prayer Father Morris held in his heart on that sunny, summer afternoon in the moments that would come be his last:

> Hail Mary, full of sorrows, the Crucified is with thee. Thou art pitiable amongst women, and pitiable is the fruit of thy womb, Jesus! Holy Mary, Mother of the Crucified, implore for us, the crucifiers of thy Son, tears of contrition, now and at the hour of our death. Amen.

Nothing would give Father Morris as much gratification as knowing that, in this book, he would leave the world a way to know and love the Blessed Virgin Mary. As we pray for the happy repose of the soul of Father Michael Morris, O.P., may our Lady hold him close and show all his beauty to the Father just as Father Morris showed all the beauty of Mary to us.

TABLE *of* CONTENTS

THE TREE OF JESSE

The Tree of Jesse,
from the *Ingeborg Psalter* (13th c.), ms. 9 fol. 14v.,
illuminated miniature, 11.8 x 7.9 in.

by an intricate network made to resemble a tree trunk with many branches and many leaves. Every person who has ever walked the earth has had some place on humanity's great family tree. Even Jesus Christ, by virtue of his Incarnation, could trace his ancestry back in human history. The Gospel of Luke inserts a genealogy of Christ that goes all the way back to Adam. The Gospel of Matthew traces the ancestry of Jesus back to the Patriarch Abraham, and links it to the line of King David. This is appropriate, for it shows Christ to be of royal lineage, a fitting bloodline for the Messiah.

The family tree of Jesus is called "The Tree of Jesse." This is because iconography draws its inspiration from the tree imagery found in the Book of the Prophet Isaiah (11:1), *A shoot shall sprout from the stump of Jesse,/ and from his roots a bud shall blossom.* Jesse was the father of King David. As early as the 2nd century Church Fathers interpreted the shoot (*virga* in Latin) with the Blessed Virgin (*virgo* in Latin). If Mary is the shoot, then Christ is the blossom, the fruit of her womb. The Virgin Mary holds a prominent position in this work. She is placed high in the middle of the page. She is crowned, enthroned, and extends her hand in blessing.

In this illuminated Jesse Tree from the 13th century, Jesus is seated between angels on the top bough of tendrils and leaves. He wears no crown. Instead, he bears the cruciform halo, symbol of his redemptive sacrifice. Seven doves surround him.

W here do we come from? Who are our ancestors? These often-asked questions are sometimes answered by the formulation of a "family tree." But family trees are often difficult to read. Spread out on paper, they form a complex geometry of names signifying relationships. Often various bloodlines are connected

Le gesse.

They represent a variety of things, from the seven sacraments to the seven gifts of the Holy Spirit. In this abbreviated and stylized family tree, the ancestors of Jesus sit beneath him. King David is there, and so is his son, Solomon. They are all connected to the couch of the sleeping Jesse, in whom God's promise is rooted. On either side stand witnesses to the fulfillment of that promise. Those on the left are three of the Evangelists (New Testament) with scrolls that paraphrase Scripture. Those on the right represent the Jews (Old Testament), who long for a Messiah and whose own prophetic tradition points to the Son of the Virgin Mary.

This Jesse Tree is a mystical tree. As such, it is not placed in an ordinary landscape. The gold-leaf background indicates that it is set in a world apart, an earthly organism serving heaven's purpose. Doves whisper into the ears of the six witnesses as they ascertain the plant's generational growth. Even the very leaves of the tree reflect the tripartite symbolism of the Trinity. Indeed this tree is like no other tree. Symbolically, it supersedes the Tree of Life and the Tree of Knowledge found in the Garden of Eden. For here this tree culminates in a bounty beyond compare, the Son of God made Man.

Art Essay November 1999

THE MEETING OF JOACHIM AND ANNE AT THE GOLDEN GATE

The Meeting of Joachim and Anne at the Golden Gate (1304–06), Giotto di Bondone (1266–1337), fresco, 78.7 x 72.8 in., Scrovegni Chapel, Padua, Italy.

I t is a rare sight in Christian art, a husband and wife kissing. The meeting of Joachim and Anne at the Golden Gate of Jerusalem is a scene of extreme rejoicing, for it is intimately connected to the birth of the Virgin Mary, destined in time to be the Mother of God. But the story that is depicted in this episode with such happiness and affection actually had its beginning in sorrow and distress.

The Gospels tell us about the birth of Jesus, but say nothing about the birth and infancy of Mary. For that, artists had to turn to the ancient and apocryphal text called the *Protoevangelium of James*. In that document it tells the story of a rich man named Joachim who was a pious Jew. He wanted to give a great offering to the Temple of Jerusalem but was forbidden to do so because he and his wife Anne had produced no offspring,

a sign to the Jews of God's disfavor. Joachim was filled with sadness and wandered straight away into the wilderness, where he pitched his tent and fasted and prayed for forty days and forty nights. Back at their home, Anne, too, lamented the situation. Her husband was gone and she shared in his shame. Even her maidservant mocked her, saying, "The Lord God has shut up your womb, to give you no fruit in Israel."

But Anne did not wallow in her sadness. She took off her mourning garments, washed her hair, and put on her wedding gown. Thus adorned, she wandered into her garden to contemplate and pray. Looking at a laurel tree, she saw a nest of sparrows. She looked at her fountain, where a school of fish swam about. She looked at the trees laden with fruit. With all these signs of life surrounding her, she pondered how it might be that she could praise the Lord as did all these bountiful wonders of nature.

Then suddenly an angel of the Lord appeared to her and said, "Anne, Anne, the Lord has heard your prayer. You shall conceive and bear, and your offspring shall be spoken of in the whole world." Exalting at this message of divine blessing, Anne promised that whether her child be male or female, she would offer it as a gift to the Lord, to serve him forever. An angel also appeared to Joachim in the wilderness to announce the good news, whereupon he rejoiced and ordered his herdsmen to gather ten lambs without blemish as

an offering to the Lord, twelve calves as an offering to the priests and elders, and a hundred baby goats as a festal sharing with the people. In the meantime, two messengers ran ahead to the city of Jerusalem to announce to Anne that her husband was returning with his flocks. She waited for him at the gate of the city. When she saw him she ran toward him, and embraced him.

And then they kissed.

In Giotto's dramatic rendition of this meeting, the robes of the two figures flow together. Joachim extends a protective arm around his wife, and Anne cradles her husband's head in her hands. The kiss fuses their two faces, and at the same time their haloes conjoin.

Even though the story continues by saying that Joachim then "rested" that first day back home with his wife, the celebrated kiss became an artistic device that would be a symbolic visual attempt to explain the sublime mystery of the Immaculate Conception. It is as if it were a spirit-filled procreative kiss between husband and wife that produced an offspring free from the stain of Original Sin. Mary's conception was debated for centuries by theologians. That she was conceived immaculately free from Original Sin by virtue of her destiny to be Christ's mother was proclaimed dogma by Pope Pius IX in the 19th century. It had long been a theological concept cherished by the Franciscan Order, with whom Giotto was attached as a lay member.

And why the Golden Gate? The story does not name the city gate at which Anne anxiously awaited her husband. But the Jews have always believed that the Messiah would come to Jerusalem through that entrance known as the Golden Gate. The artist has painted the arch in the color gold. Prophecy and fulfillment are embedded in the picture. Here the grandmother and grandfather of the Messiah embrace with marital affection as a party of smiling ladies looks on. Perhaps they are some of Anne's more faithful and sympathetic servants. But the woman in black who wears no smile, who turns away, could she be the servant who ridiculed Anne? Or is she perhaps a figurative omen of their daughter, who will experience much happiness as the Mother of the Lord but will also experience many sorrows as the "Mater Dolorosa," a woman whose heart will be pierced with sadness?

Art Essay July 2001

THE VIRGIN OF THE IMMACULATE CONCEPTION

The Virgin of the Immaculate Conception (1618–19), Diego Velázquez (1599–1660), oil on canvas, 53.1 x 40 in.

There she stands, a maiden of twelve or thirteen years of age. Her hands are folded in prayer, and she is crowned with stars. Beneath her feet is the moon, while luminescent clouds frame her body. This is a mystical Madonna, inspired by Saint John's vision of a woman clothed with the sun in the Book of Revelation. It is a solemnly beautiful depiction of Mary in her guise as the Immaculate Conception. But behind the comeliness of the painting lay centuries of sometimes cantankerous debate and papal interjections while theology, politics, nationalism, and popular piety all collided to create the birthing pangs of an idea that could be understood as truth only through the progress of time.

The question that sparked the debate concerned the holiness of Mary, whom the Council of Ephesus called the "Mother of God" in AD 431. It was granted that she was indeed holy (and referred to as such in Scripture), but the question remained to what degree, and when this holiness began. It was contended that Mary, having been predestined from the beginning as the Woman through whom Christ and his divine nature would be made manifest on earth, would be presumably exempt from all sin, even from the original taint inherited from Adam. Through the first Eve all died, but through the "second Eve" (who is Mary) all are made alive. Belief that Mary was made holy from the moment of her conception began to take hold in the East by the 8th or 9th century, and a feast that celebrated her in that respect reached the West by the 11th century. The Immaculate Conception is not taught explicitly in Scripture, but explicit belief arose in the Church's understanding of it as it unfolded itself through the ages, prompted by the Holy Spirit through meditation and rational debate. That Mary's virginity was preserved even as God called her to motherhood is itself striking evidence of how her vocation was assisted by divine grace.

Understanding God's plan for her and the whole human race prompted scholastic theologians of the 13th century to grapple with serious questions. If Mary was conceived without sin, wouldn't that mean that she was exempt from Christ's redemption? Would it not be more proper and correct to think of her as conceived in sin but sanctified with divine grace while gestating in the womb of her mother? Thomas Aquinas felt this was the case. The Dominicans followed his lead, while the Franciscans followed that of Duns Scotus. He argued that Mary above all others was in need of Christ's redemption, for only by his merits could she possibly be free from contracting Original Sin at the moment of her conception. For a long time the papacy allowed the debate to continue. By the late 15th century Pope Sixtus IV forbade either side from accusing the other of heresy. But he also approved an

Office for the feast. In Counter-Reformation Spain especially there was a groundswell advocating the belief in the Immaculate Conception, and its cause became part of the national identity. The Spanish crown continually lobbied the popes to proclaim it as dogma, and Spanish artists in the 17th century created numerous and exquisite works of art on the subject.

This is one of those paintings produced in the Golden Age of Spanish art. Velázquez was still a teenager when he painted it for the Carmelites of Seville, who were known for their passionate arguments in favor of the Immaculate Conception. The iconography of the Immaculate Conception became standardized over time and codified in 1649 by the painter Francisco Pacheco, who was the artistic censor for the Inquisition. There are some who believe that the model for this Madonna is in fact the daughter of Pacheco, Juana, whom Velázquez married around the same time as he painted the picture. The rules that Pacheco established for representing the Immaculate Conception may have been partially influenced by his son-in-law's earlier representation of it: the source was to be the Book of Revelation (12:1), Mary was to be painted in the first spring of youth with grave sweet eyes and golden hair; her hands were to be folded on her bosom or joined in prayer; there was to be a flood of light around her, and twelve stars were to form a crown over her head while the moon beneath her feet was to be illuminated from above.

The painting may also have been commissioned to celebrate a recent decree of Pope Paul V that declared the opposing opinion against the Immaculate Conception the "less pious opinion." This sparked celebrations throughout Spain, especially in Seville, where it was marked by fireworks, carnivals, tournaments, and bullfights. In Granada some Dominican friars were injured as a result of the public response. Despite growing enthusiasm for the papacy to declare the Immaculate Conception a dogma, Rome remained cautious. Pope Gregory XV declared, "The Holy Spirit, although besought by most constant prayers, has not yet opened to his Church the secrets of this mystery." Two more centuries elapsed until a flurry of supportive activity occurred in the 19th century. The Miraculous Medal apparitions took place in 1830, and in 1846 the American bishops at the Council of Baltimore declared the Immaculate Conception the patroness of the United States.

Finally, in 1854 Pope Pius IX defined as dogma the doctrine "which upholds that the most Blessed Virgin Mary was preserved from all stain of Original Sin in the first instant of her conception, by a singular grace and privilege of Almighty God, in consideration of the merits of Jesus Christ, Savior of the human race…."

Heaven approved.

Just four years later in a grotto in Lourdes, France, "a lady" appeared to a peasant girl named Bernadette Soubirous, and she identified herself by saying, "I am the Immaculate Conception."

THE PRESENTATION
OF THE VIRGIN
IN THE TEMPLE

The Presentation of the Virgin in the Temple (1534–38)
Titian (c. 1490–1576),
oil on canvas, 135.8 x 305.4 in.

The steps leading to the Temple of Jerusalem are long and steep. She ascends them with an elegance and grace far beyond her years. An aureole surrounds her as she holds her light blue gown and proceeds forward with alacrity. She raises her arm toward the waiting high priest.

This is the Presentation of the Virgin Mary in the Temple, an event not recorded in the Bible but found in that ancient text known as the *Protoevangelium of James*. In the document, the birth and childhood of the Virgin Mary is recounted. The legend records that her parents, Joachim and Anne, had prayed for a child to grace their marriage. When an angel appeared to Anne to announce to her that she would at last give birth and that the child would be blessed throughout the whole world, Anne was so overjoyed that she vowed to present the child

as an offering to the Lord. She fulfilled that vow when the child was three years old. In doing so an ancient symbolism was renewed: Mary, the Ark of the New Covenant, was thus brought into the temple in the same way as Moses was instructed to place the Ark of the Testimony inside the Tent of Meeting (Ex 40:21).

"Let us invite the daughters of Israel, and they shall take each a taper or a lamp, and attend on her, that the child may not turn back from the Temple of the Lord," declared her father Joachim. And when they came to the Temple, they placed her on the first step, and she ascended them alone, never looking back. The high priest received her and blessed her and exclaimed, "Mary, the Lord has magnified your name to all generations, and in you shall be made known the redemption of the children of Israel." He then led her to the altar, and once she was placed there she danced with her feet, so that all the house of Israel rejoiced with her, and loved her.

This consecration of Mary to the service of the Temple has been a favorite theme in western art, particularly in nunneries. Although the legend says that Mary was only three years old when she was presented, some artists have portrayed her older, veiled, and with a taper in her hand, looking very much like a young nun. But Titian has remained faithful to the legend, and the strong architectural emphasis of the staircase makes the diminutive Mary look heroic for trying to scale them.

Traditionally, artists have included fifteen steps for the young Mary to climb. This is because of a passage found in Josephus, who said that in the Temple "between the wall which separated the men from the women, and the great porch…were fifteen steps." This was a symbolic construction to evoke the memory of the fifteen psalms recited by the children of Israel as they returned from exile and caught their first glimpse of the Temple. But Titian has only approximated fifteen. He included one more, and broke the stairs up into three sections: one of eight steps, one of five, and one of three. Iconographers speculate that the tripartite division is a Trinitarian symbol (and the last three steps leading into the sanctuary are equally Trinitarian). Mathematicians see the ratio between the numbers 8, 5, and 13 as a

reference to the Golden Mean found in Renaissance humanist symbolism. Still, others point to the young girl resting her hands on the fourth and fifth steps, thereby breaking with her two hands the lower staircase into sections of five and three. The numbers 1, 1, 2, 3, 5, 8, and 13 (in which each number is the sum of its predecessors) thus figure into the painting and reflect the logorhythmic spiral, an order of growth found in nature and written about by Medieval mathematicians.

Less arcane and much more symbolically obvious in this stage-setting of heavy architectural verticals and horizontals is the diagonal break of

the staircase itself, which is lit in such a way as to lead the eye upward with Mary's ascent. The mutilated classical sculpture of a torso, nestled in the lower right corner of the painting, is a reference to the decline of the pagan world. Likewise, the haggard and tired old woman selling ritual offerings at the Temple steps represents an exhausted and yet persistent Judaism. In contrast, the noble figures of Anne—(decked in white) and Joachim (with red tunic and dark stole) stand erect and watch with regal dignity the ascent of their daughter into the Temple of the Lord. They represent the continuity between the Jewish and the Christian worlds. Titian included a self-portrait in his rendering of Joachim, and painted several other portraits of friends and officials in the Scuola della Carita, which occupied the present Academia building. Set over two doorframes, the painting has never left the space for which it was intended.

Until she was deemed to be ready for a husband, the legend states that Mary remained in the Temple for ten years, where she became an example of every virtue. She was industrious, wise, temperate, and chaste. What is particularly significant in this painting by Titian is the fact that it is one of the few heroic renderings of a young girl in the history of art. But, is that not appropriate for the one who was called "blessed" and destined to be the Mother of God?

Art Essay November 2003

THE MARRIAGE
OF THE VIRGIN

The Marriage of the Virgin (aka *Sposalizio*) (1504),
Raphael (1483–1520),
oil on panel, 66.9 x 46.4 in.

According to these sources, Mary's youth in the Temple passed quickly. She took a vow of virginity there and had become the *persona maxissima grata*, sanctified and sanctifying. But when she turned twelve (some sources claim fourteen) the priests of the Temple felt that she should leave the sacred precincts and find a husband. Assuming a parental role, the chief priest donned his ceremonial vestment with twelve bells and entered the sanctuary praying for guidance in a choosing a husband for Mary. An angel appeared to him and instructed him to assemble the widowers of the people. Each should each bring a rod, over which the Lord would provide a miraculous sign on the man destined to be her husband.

The announcement went out and the ram's horns sounded from the parapets of the Temple. Single men came running with staves in their hands. Joseph the carpenter threw down his axe and joined them as they assembled before the high priest. He took their staves into the Temple and prayed. After a while he returned to the men and gave each staff back to its owner. Joseph's rod flowered and a dove flew over his head. The high priest then said to him, "Joseph, to you has fallen the good fortune to receive the virgin of the Lord: take her under your care."

The artist Raphael depicts here the marriage of the Virgin, with the high priest presiding as Joseph slips a ring on her finger and the Temple dominating the background. In *Pseudo–Matthew* it states that

W here Scripture is silent, artists looked to the Apocrypha for inspiration. While it is recorded in the Gospel that Mary was betrothed to a man named Joseph, the story of how this came about is not mentioned. It is explained, however, in the *Golden Legend*, a 13th-century compendium which itself drew upon a variety of non-canonical sources like the *Protoevangelium of James* and the *Gospel of Pseudo–Matthew*.

Mary was assigned five virgins to accompany her to Joseph's home–Rebecca, Zipporah, Suzanna, Abigail, and Cael–where together they spun colored wools while Joseph returned to his vocation as an itinerant carpenter. Thus, for a time, Mary spent her time in the company of women with no man near her.

In Raphael's painting those contenders who were not selected to be Mary's husband stand behind Joseph as grooms. One sore loser breaks his rod over his knee. Joseph is depicted as neither young nor old, his age being a controversy that worked itself out in the visual arts as the centuries progressed. The figures of Mary and the high priest and Joseph dominate the foreground. They gently respond to the balance of the space with the delicate tilting of their heads. Raphael imbued the painting with a symbolic numerology. Five virgins and five grooms accompany Mary and Joseph, constituting twelve figures, equal to the number of Apostles and the number of the signs in the zodiac. With the high priest they number thirteen, equaling that of Christ and his disciples. The Temple is depicted in such a way that we see twelve of its columns and seven of its sides. Seven is the number of the sacraments, of the gifts of the Holy Spirit, and the Christian communities addressed by Saint John. Raphael was well aware of the sacred numbers and harmonies that permeate the Judeo-Christian world as well as the classical world of Plato and Pythagoras.

Had the Temple design that Raphael represents here been actually constructed, it would have been one of the architectural masterpieces of the Renaissance. As it is, Raphael's painting was an exercise in proving his ability to overshadow his teacher Perugino, who had designed a similar painting of lesser quality a short time before. This was Raphael's masterpiece up to that point in his career. He was only twenty years old.

THE ANNUNCIATION

The Annunciation (1450–53),
Fra Filippo Lippi (c. 1406–1469),
egg tempera on wood, 27 x 60.1 in.

I n a garden close, an angel with peacock wings genuflects before the Virgin Mary. This is Gabriel, Archangel of the Annunciation, who brings a message of blessing to the maiden who is destined to be the Mother of God. He holds a lily, symbol of purity. His haloed head bends forward and he gazes through the threshold of Mary's private chamber.

Rejoice, O highly favored one! The Lord is with you, are his first words of greeting (cf. Lk 1:28).

When one is visited by an angel, the first response seems to be one of fear. This prompts the angel immediately to reassure her: *Mary, do not be afraid; you have won God's favor* (cf. Lk 1:30).

Gabriel has been sent by God to deliver a message. The very word "angel" means messenger. As such, he acts as a divine ambassador. He raises his right hand in blessing. It mimics the same gesture found in the hand of God piercing through the dark shadowy vapor above.

Listen! You are to conceive and bear a son, and you must name him Jesus. He will be great and will be called Son of the Most High (cf. Lk 1:31-32a).

How could this be, questioned Mary, for she was a virgin. The angel reassured her of God's miraculous ability to make this happen: *The Holy Spirit will come upon you and the power of the Most High will cover you with its shadow* (cf. Lk 1:35).

I am the handmaid of the Lord, replied Mary. *Let it be done to me as you have said* (cf. Lk 1:38).

Here in Fra Filippo Lippi's painting, the symbolism of virginity undefiled is subtly maintained. A pot of lilies acts as a barricade between the inside

chamber and the outside world. The sealed sanctity of her bedroom acts a metaphor for her inviolate body. Only the Divine can penetrate this inner sanctum. Her role in God's plan is Trinitarian. Mary is the daughter of the Father, the mother of the Son, and the bride of the Holy Spirit. The angel is not the agent of this miraculous conception. That is the work of the Holy Spirit, who is shown in serial images progressing downward toward the Virgin's swollen abdomen, where there is a small opening in her dress emitting rays of gold. Mary's head is bent downward in humility. She has accepted God's plan. The spark of life has begun inside her. The Virgin's womb has become a sanctuary, her body an ostensorium. The chair on which she sits is now a throne. Not by chance has the Carmelite artist draped the back of her chair with material that looks like a humeral veil, a liturgical shawl with which priests wrap their shoulders, arms, and hands as they carry a monstrance enshrining a consecrated host and offer benediction.

Mary has become the New Ark of the Covenant. With her *fiat* the Church celebrates her pregnancy. In approximately nine months' time, the solemnity of Christ's Nativity will be observed. And soon the celebration of her Visitation with her cousin Elizabeth will be honored. But for now, for this feast and its representation here in this painting, in the quiet corner of her room, the Virgin Mary peers down and contemplates the spark of divine life now growing within her.

THE VISITATION

The Visitation (c. 1505), Hans and/or Jakob Strüb (16th c.), oil on panel, 31.4 x 21.5 in.

T he Feast of the Visitation is an occasion for the celebration of Motherhood in the most mystical sense, for it was due to the maternity of two women that the long-awaited Messianic age was ushered into history. In Sacred Scripture, Luke's account of the Annunciation to Mary, the news that she was to be the Mother of Jesus, so filled her with happiness that she hurried to visit her cousin Elizabeth to share in that joy. The angel Gabriel had told Mary that her aged cousin was also pregnant, *for nothing is impossible to God* (cf. Lk 1:37). Filled with the Holy Spirit, Mary's journey from Nazareth to the hill country of Judah was one of motion-filled exultation. The vocabulary used in Scripture supports this: Mary left her home *in haste* (Lk 1:39), and as soon as she greeted Elizabeth the babe in her cousin's womb *leapt for joy* (cf. Lk 1:41). Elizabeth in turn greeted Mary with *a loud cry* (cf. Lk 1:42), and Mary responded with a hymn of praise to God, thereafter known as the *Magnificat*.

In this painting, which used to be part of a much larger altarpiece in an Augustinian convent, the figures of Mary and Elizabeth embrace. Both women are veiled, yet three sections of the younger Mary's long and lustrous hair cascade down over her shoulder. As Elizabeth stares into Mary's eyes she sees that the Virgin's sight is fixed on something otherworldly. Mary has become intimately connected to the Trinitarian Godhead. Mary's hand extends to Elizabeth's arm, but it is painted in such a way that her long and faceted fingers seem to tingle with excitement.

Overpaintings on the robes of both women were discovered in 1987 when this panel was submitted to infrared reflectography. When the paint was removed, it revealed fully intact figures of the unborn Christ and John the Baptist within the protruding abdomens of Mary and Elizabeth. Depictions like this are rare in art, and while a later owner must have found it unseemly and had them painted over, the artist who conceived this work wanted to show in a visual way the miraculous interaction that Scripture says took place between those children in the womb. The figure of Christ stands radiant in a nimbus, while the figure of John the Baptist is in a position of worship before his divine cousin. In Scripture (cf. Lk 1:42-44) Elizabeth is filled with the Holy Spirit, and she exclaims to Mary: *Of all women you are the most blessed, and blessed is the fruit of your womb. Why should I be honored with a visit from the mother of my Lord? For the moment your greeting reached my ears, the child in my womb leapt for joy.*

Thus, for the first time in Luke's Gospel, Jesus is called *Lord*, and his Messiahship is confirmed by the mother of the figure who would one day herald Christ as the *Lamb of God*. Mary herself is exalted in this address. She has indeed become the New Ark of the Covenant, for the presence of the Living God grows within her womb. The profound symbolism between Mary and the Ark unfolds itself during the Visitation. Just as King David once queried, *How can the ark of the LORD come to me?* when it was approaching Jerusalem (2 Sm 6:9), so, too, when Mary approaches the hill country near Jerusalem, Elizabeth asks the same question. Just as King David danced for joy before the Ark, so too John the Baptist leapt in joy in the womb of Elizabeth as Mary came near. Mary's coming to the house of Elizabeth and staying for three months was considered a blessing, just as the repose of the Ark in the house of Obededom (2 Sm 6:11) for three months brought blessings to that family.

Tradition holds that Mary met Elizabeth at a well in a little village not far from Jerusalem called Ain Karem. In the painting the event takes place outdoors, signified by the hillock in the background and the grass-edged path beneath their feet. Elizabeth has just stepped out of her house. The artist has kept the details of the landscape and the costumes to a minimum. The primary purpose of the painting is to portray a religious event, and because this event is an important moment in salvation history, commemorated as the second mystery of the most holy rosary, the scene is embellished in gold. Mary concluded her greeting of Elizabeth by singing a song of praise to God (Lk 1:46b-55): *My soul proclaims the greatness of the Lord;/ my spirit rejoices in God my savior./ For he has looked with favor on his lowly servant....* The dithyramb continues as an ode to God's goodness to his people. Her song is filled with the faith and hope of Israel and of the salvific promise fulfilled. Because Mary is also a symbol of the Church, her song of praise becomes our own. Because she is the Mother of God, we reverence her and fulfill that prediction made long ago when the *Magnificat* was first uttered, *From now on, all generations will call me blessed* (cf. Lk 1:48).

Art Essay May 2001

THE NATIVITY

The Nativity (c. 1400),
Anonymous artist of the Meuse-Rhineland,
tempera on panel, 12.9 x 8.2 in.

One can take the traditional Nativity scene for granted and overlook the subtle changes in detail that bring new meaning to an old art form. Such is the case of this panel painting, executed by an unknown Dutch artist around 1400.

No stable is represented here. The birth of Christ would seem at first to be taking place in a wooded ravine under an open sky. However, a more probable interpretation of the womb-like chasm is that it is the artist's suggestion of a cave. The presence of tethered livestock would imply that this is at the very least a sanctuary of refuge where the divinely ordained event can take place. God the Father, surrounded by azure cherubs, imparts his blessing from above. Like an icon divorced from time and space and placed in a mystical realm of burnished gold, this Nativity is not site-specific. The town of Bethlehem cannot be seen in the distance, nor are there shepherds in the background tending their flocks. Nature is indeed present, but in a strictly symbolic way.

For instance, the mat on which Mary reclines is covered with a design showing sheaves of corn. The cornhusks splay out as if they were fleurs-de-lis, the symbol of the lily that is sacred to the Virgin and a sign of purity. But corn itself plays an important role in an apocryphal tale of the Holy Family. According to that story, when they were later fleeing from Herod's soldiers and heading for safety in Egypt, they passed a farmer sowing corn in his field. Mary asked the farmer that if soldiers should ask him if he saw a family racing toward Egypt, he should tell them that indeed he saw them just as he was beginning to sow his corn. At the end of the day, the farmer finished his sowing and went to bed. Later the next morning the soldiers did indeed show up and asked the farmer if he had seen the family in flight. He said yes, they had passed by when he first started planting in the field. The soldiers looked at the field and saw fully mature stalks of corn standing there. Unaware of the miracle that had taken place, the soldiers estimated that the family had a twelve-week head start and abandoned their pursuit. Thus corn takes on a protective symbolism here, and at the same time points to the dangers that lie ahead. Elsewhere in Europe the story substituted corn with wheat. In fact, the Magyars believed that every kernel of wheat contained within it an imprint of the Madonna and

Child. Here sheaves of wheat radiate from the Virgin's mat as if they were rays of light flowing from a mandorla. Wheat is used in making Eucharistic bread, and thus the symbolism continues in a sacramental mode, especially in the manger where the incarnate Christ has been laid on a bed of wheat sheaves.

Not only does the mat with corn designs point to other stories yet to unfold, it acts formally as a device that divides the painting in two. In the lower left of the painting, we see that Mary has turned her back on the Christ Child and faces Joseph. This is unusual in Nativity scenes, where the Virgin is customarily represented as the first to adore her newborn. But here she seems to be mentally engaged in the activity of Joseph, who has taken one of his stockings and is splitting it apart in order to make warm swaddling clothes for Jesus. Not only does the action attest to the poverty of the Holy Family; it casts both Mary and Joseph in the role of loving and protective parents of the Child, anticipating at every step the dangers that await him.

In the upper right of the painting, the ox and the ass and a midwife reverence and care for the unclad Jesus. This sector of the painting exudes peaceful repose, but it is not without its controversy. The stark nudity in which the Child is represented made later theologians uneasy, as the Renaissance increasingly engaged in such expositions. But devotional prudishness could not outweigh the dogmatic fact that Christ took on human flesh wholly and entirely. The painter extolled this fact in a way that the preacher and the priest could not.

That the painting relies heavily on apocryphal sources is evident by the presence of a midwife who is not mentioned in Scripture, but does appear in the ancient *Protoevangelium of James*. And while the ox and ass do not show up in the Gospels, they do in a Hebrew text of Habakkuk wherein the Messiah will be known between two beasts, and again in Isaiah (1:3) where it says *An ox knows its owner, and an ass, its master's manger*. Symbolically, the beasts represent whole nations of peoples. The ox represents the Gentiles and the donkey represents the Jews. Here both animals hover over the Child and are ready to lick him with their warm tongues lest he catch cold.

Drawing upon ancient legends and the symbolism in which Christians imbued their iconography, this Nativity celebrates not only the human figures of the story but incorporates flora and fauna, too, making all of creation bless the Lord.

THE NATIVITY

The Nativity (c. 1430),
Robert Campin (1375–1444),
oil on panel, 33.8 x 28.3 in.

Christmas is a time for storytelling, and in this Netherlandish painting we discover that not all the tales surrounding Christ's birth are to be found exclusively in the Bible. Through the centuries, artists have drawn upon a vast body of apocryphal stories, some of them nearly as old as the Gospels themselves, using them as a source for pictorial inspiration to supplement what we know of Christ's Birth from Sacred Scripture.

The *Protoevangelium of James*, an apocryphal text dated by some scholars to have been written as early as AD 150, is the source of many images dealing with the girlhood of the Virgin Mary, her betrothal to Joseph, and the birth of Jesus. Here in Campin's *Nativity* he has included the tale incorporated in that text of a midwife whom Joseph calls to aid Mary in her delivery in Bethlehem. The midwife, whose back is to the viewer of the painting, arrived in time to marvel at the miraculous birth, which the *Protoevangelium* says took place within an enveloping cloud followed by a burst of light. Her friend, named Salome, arrived

too late to see the wondrous event take place. She refused to believe the midwife's account of how this holy Virgin gave birth to a child. Like the Doubting Thomas of Scripture, Salome declared that she would only believe if she could subject the claim to a physical examination. In attempting to touch the Virgin, however, Salome's hand was consumed by fire and it began to wither. In great distress, she prayed to God for forgiveness. Thereupon an angel appeared who instructed her to touch the Christ Child and be healed. Here in the painting she has already done this and she extends her palm forward to show those around her how her hand—and her faith in God—have been restored.

The story of the midwife and Salome exemplifies in the painting the contrast between belief and disbelief. In both the apocryphal and the scriptural accounts of the Nativity, belief is sparked through the agency of angels. Three angels hover over the stable in this picture. They have informed the shepherds tending their flocks of Christ's birth (Lk 2:8-18). The shepherds enter the scene through a Dutch door and stand in awe at the sight of the newborn Child. Joseph, whose own doubts about Mary's pregnancy were quelled by the testimony of an angel, genuflects before the naked Child and holds a lighted candle. It is an unusual depiction for the foster father of Jesus, one that is not drawn from the pages of Scripture. Instead, the artist was inspired by the revelations of the late 14th-century mystic Saint Bridget of Sweden.

Specific details from her vision of Christ's Birth were also incorporated in his painting: the Virgin, dressed in white, has removed her veil and kneels before her Son, who is placed naked on the ground; Joseph too adores Jesus and provides Mary with the light-giving taper. But, as Saint Bridget related in her vision, neither the sun nor Joseph's candle could compare with the brilliance of the Child's spiritual aura, which surpassed all material light. Jesus, the Light of the World, reclines on a paten of radiating beams in Campin's painting. Jesus is the new manna from heaven now lying on the earth (Jn 6:51). According to Saint Bridget's vision, the Virgin swaddled the Christ Child and placed him in the manger after having welcomed him as "my God, and my Lord, and my Son."

Behind the Holy Family, an ass and an ox share the stable. They are fixtures in every Nativity creche, yet their presence at the scene is not mentioned in the Gospels. Tradition has placed them there because they fulfill a Messianic prophecy of the prophet Isaiah (1:3), *The ox knows its owner, and an ass, his master's manger*. Not until the 8th or 9th century does one find an account that mentions the beasts being present at the manger, and that is described in the apocryphal account known as the *Gospel of Pseudo-Matthew*.

All in all, this Nativity scene by Robert Campin is a picture puzzle put together with pieces drawn from various literary sources. It gives witness to the enduring wonder and delight exhibited by Christians as they relate in diverse ways the mysterious and awe-inspiring event that occurred two thousand years ago, the fact that God took on flesh and became man.

THE ADORATION OF THE SHEPHERDS

The Adoration of the Shepherds (1505–10), Giorgione (c. 1477–1510), oil on panel, 35.7 x 43.5 in.

His name is synonymous with mystery. He never signed his paintings. None of them are dated. But in his short career—a mere twenty years—Giorgione sparked a revolution on canvas by creating a new pictorial technique in which landscape was infused with poetry and mysticism.

In his painting *The Adoration of the Shepherds*, the composition appears to be divided in two, with a cluster of human figures assembled on one side and an idealized landscape balancing the other half. On the right side is a traditional scene of the Nativity, with the adoring shepherds approaching the cave and falling on their knees before the Christ Child. It has the same elements as those depicted so many times in the Middle Ages and echoed into the Renaissance. Joseph is older than Mary. His shock of white beard, a symbol of old age, is as illuminated as is Mary's white veil, a symbol of her virginity. Often, in Medieval paintings, Joseph is old and querulous, off to the side and sleeping, or still wondering what this great mystery is all about. But he is devoutly worshiping here. Not until Teresa of Ávila, who had a great devotion to Saint Joseph, do we start to find the carpenter depicted by artists as younger and more vigorous.

The shepherds wear tattered clothing. Theirs is a life of poverty. Likewise, the Christ Child is depicted naked and lying on the ground as a sign that he came into the world in poverty. In Saint Bridget of Sweden's mystical vision of the Nativity, she said that she saw the Virgin place Jesus on the bare earth and that she kneeled to adore him. This account had a great impact on artists and it is reflected in Giorgione's painting. It also is a foreshadowing of Christ's Death, wherein he will be laid on the ground and hastily prepared for burial. The Word has assumed human flesh in order to redeem the world.

And yet, this world is one in which Giorgione takes great delight in painting. He places the Nativity in a luscious landscape that harkens back to Greek poetry and the simple joys of Arcadia. Despite the poverty of their condition, the Holy Family and the shepherds are placed in a pastoral setting that exudes peace and quiet. Even the ox and ass are kept at bay, hidden within the shadows

of the cave. Furthermore, there are no noisy angels here, singing or playing musical instruments. The artist has sparingly painted a few cherub heads over the entrance to the cave. Their presence testifies to the miracle of the event without disturbing the sweet silence of Nature in solemn repose.

Giorgione's painting departs on several points from the Infancy Narrative found in Gospel of Luke, but when he does so it is for the sake of a higher symbolism. In Luke's account angels appear to the shepherds and tell them to rush to Bethlehem to see the Messiah, whom they will identify as an *infant wrapped in swaddling clothes* (Lk 2:12). In Giorgione's rendition the Baby Jesus appears naked in order to emphasize the reality of the Incarnation. In Luke's Gospel it says that the angels appeared to the shepherds who were *living in the fields and keeping the night watch over their flock* (Lk 2:8). But in this painting the announcement to the shepherds and their subsequent adoration do not take place at night. The atmosphere is as bright and as clear as the day. In this case it would seem that Giorgione's painting harkens instead to the Gospel of John, wherein Christ is described as *the true light, which enlightens everyone* (Jn 1:9).

If Christ is the Light of the World, then our life's journey becomes a pilgrimage toward that light in much the same way as the Star of Bethlehem guided the Magi on their voyage. Giorgione's landscape is imbued with the notion of pilgrimage. Not only are the shepherds dressed like pilgrims, with their hats and walking staffs; the meandering country road behind them exalts in the notion

of journey. Far distant mountains unite with the sky in a veil of bluish haze, but the more proximate hills show signs of pleasant domesticity with architectural elements dotting the countryside. A river of clear water zigzags and pools through the plain, recalling the words of Christ to the Samaritan woman, *Whoever drinks the water I shall give will never thirst; the water I shall give will become in him a spring of water welling up to eternal life* (Jn 4:14). The artist has water flowing most clearly in the tiny ravine where the shepherds are shown tending their sheep. An angel, almost hidden in the trees above them, proclaims the birth of Christ. It is as if the artist did not want the supernal powers to overwhelm the landscape. Nature herself is rejoicing here, and it is a pleasure to behold.

THE SEED OF DAVID

The Seed of David (1858–64),
Dante Gabriel Rossetti (1828–1882),
triptych, oil on canvas,
central panel 90 x 60 in., each wing 73 x 24.5 in.,
Llandaff Cathedral, Cardiff, Wales

One of the most striking characteristics of Pre-Raphaelite painting, the mid-19th-century English art movement that sought to revitalize art in the manner of the Italian painters prior to Raphael, is the ability to take an old religious theme and make it seem fresh and new. Certainly the New Testament is replete with references to Christ being a descendent of David. But, with the exception of the Tree of Jesse motif in western Medieval art, there are few moments in history when painters explored that idea with new depth and originality.

This was the theme chosen by Dante Gabriel Rossetti, the founder of the Pre-Raphaelite Brotherhood, when he was given the commission to paint a triptych for the restoration of the Anglican Llandaff Cathedral. It was a difficult commission for the artist. Certainly he had painted smaller religious subjects before, particularly Marian themes, with masterful facility. But this was to be a large-scale work, over ninety inches tall in some places. Such a commission was unusual for its period. And while the Pre-Raphaelites painted a large number of religious works, rarely did they end up in churches.

In the six long years it took Rossetti to paint this triptych he came into conflict with the commissioners who wanted him to paint an image that was lighter and more decorative. To mollify their wishes the artist went so far as to suggest that the area around the triptych be painted black! Despite the disagreements and the difficulties, the resulting work satisfied the intention of the commissioners, who wanted the piece to reflect equality of all human beings in the eyes of God. Where else but in church can high and low, rich and poor, monarch and peasant, come together as equals as they worship their Lord?

In a letter to his aunt, Rossetti explained what his intentions were in the formulation of the painting. The primary purpose of the work was to show how Christ sprang from both high and low in the person of David, who was both a shepherd and a king. Thus in the wings of the triptych David is portrayed in each of those roles. On the left panel he is seen as a shepherd boy with a sling, walking forward to meet Goliath, as the Israelite army watches him from behind in their protective entrenchment. On the right panel David is seen wearing a crown and seated on a peacock throne as he plays the harp. "Accordingly in the center-piece," wrote the artist, "an angel is represented leading the shepherd and king to worship in the stable at the feet of Christ,

who is in his mother's arms. She holds his hand for the shepherd and his foot for the king, to kiss—so showing the superiority of poverty over riches in the eyes of Christ; while the one lays his crook, the other his crown, at the Savior's feet. There is an opening all round the stable through which angels are looking in, while other angels are playing on musical instruments in a loft above."

To better explain the iconography to worshipers in the cathedral, Rossetti composed the following poem to accompanyt the piece:

Christ sprang from David Shepherd,
   and even so
From David King, being born of high and low.
The shepherd lays his crook,
   the King his crown
Here at Christ's feet, and high and low
   bow down.

For his models Rossetti chose friends and associates. The head of the mature King David is based on William Morris, the celebrated genius of the Arts and Crafts Movement in England. The Child Jesus was modeled on the baby daughter of Pre-Raphaelite painter Arthur Hughes. The face of the shepherd David is thought by some to be an image of the artist Edward Burne-Jones, while others claim that it is a portrait of an acquaintance who was a mechanic. And in 1861, Rossetti replaced his original model for the Virgin (Ruth Herbert) with Jane Morris, the wife of William Morris. Above all others, Jane Morris became the paradigm of Pre-Raphaelite beauty, with her languorous poses and long, flowing hair. Rossetti had always believed that there was no greater exemplar of female excellence than the Virgin Mary. But there was another reason, besides beauty, for which Rossetti decided

to have Jane Morris model as the Holy Mother. Earlier that year, Jane and William Morris's first child was born, and Rossetti felt it appropriate that his model for Mary have the same experience of loving motherhood with her newborn as did Mary with Jesus. This feeling of intense love is generated in the central panel of the adoration scene, as the Virgin lifts the child gently upward toward her cheek. The close bond between Mother and Child is further reflected in the nearby attendant angels, one of whom grabs Mary around the waist in a loving embrace while the other tenderly grasps the hand of the kneeling king. This daisy chain of tactile love is a modern phenomenon, one that was practiced often by the Pre-Raphaelites in their depiction of the Holy Family.

While good art aspires to goodness, beauty, and truth, real life doesn't always live up to the same lofty principles. In the history of art, many a painter had had his mistress pose as the Virgin Mary, and that tradition would continue in this painting. While Jane and William Morris loved their children, their marriage suffered from a certain chronic ambivalence. Ten years after this triptych was completed, Rossetti began an affair with Jane Morris, while her husband took off to pursue various political and artistic projects. It is interesting to note that unlike the preparatory watercolor sketch for this painting, the figure of Saint Joseph has been eliminated. The nuclear family, so central to society and celebrated in religion with the image of the Holy Family, is not represented in this cathedral triptych. In the painting, Jane Morris, in dreamy self-absorption, lifts the beloved child to her cheek with her back to her real-life husband. And he, posing as the artist King, barricades his head against her as he lifts the instrument of his art up against his own cheek.

If art imitates life, can the opposite also be said? Can life imitate art? If so, then this triptych is a portent of things to come for those who had collaborated at the outset with nothing but the highest intentions.

THE ADORATION OF THE MAGI

The Adoration of the Magi (c. 1494),
Hieronymus Bosch (c. 1450–1516),
triptych, oil on panel and grisaille, 58 x 66.3 in.

F ew painters are skilled enough to infuse their work with so many fascinating layers of symbolism as the mysterious artist Hieronymus Bosch. His triptych of the *Adoration of the Magi* is at once an imposing composition resplendent with exotic images. He set his figures in the foreground low on the picture plane and posed them as if they were frozen in time. But a closer inspection of this painting reveals it to be a conveyor of deeper meanings, not all of them peaceful, some of them disturbing.

In the central panel the Three Wise Men appear in the conventional depiction of the three ages of man: youth, the prime of life, and old age. Bosch has given young Caspar the appearance of an Ethiopian, a fashionable device representing the ethnographic consciousness that was popular at the end of the 15th century, when European explorers discovered cultures far different from their own. The introduction of the black magus added a symbolic scope to the Adoration of the Christ Child imagery, for each wise man now represented a continent. They were Africa, Asia, and Europe bringing gifts to the wondrous Child of Bethlehem. They also bring prophecies for the Infant based on typological symbolism that unites the past with the present and the future. Melchior (Europe) has pride of place as he kneels before the Madonna and Child, set apart by a wooden post that supports the ramshackle porch as if it were a rustic baldachin. He has placed his gift of gold before the King of kings. On it are sculpted figures of Abraham about to sacrifice Isaac on Mount Moriah, an Old Testament prefiguration of Christ's sacrifice on Calvary. Balthazar (Asia) fittingly offers frankincense to the Child Jesus. His prophecy is embroidered on his shoulder cape, which shows the Queen of Sheba seeking the wisdom of Solomon, a prefiguration of the Magi's own journey. Furthermore, the composition of the Virgin with the Christ Child seated in her lap has been called the "Seat of Wisdom" since Medieval times, thus enriching the interpretation. The African Caspar, elegantly costumed in white, bears a silver goblet of myrrh for the Savior, an ointment to be administered at his death. Its lid is embellished with an allusion to the value of sacrifice

Jheronimus bosch

in a scene taken from the Second Book of Samuel (23:15-17). King David craved to drink the water of Bethlehem, which was then brought to him by three of his bravest warriors, who broke through enemy lines to obtain it. Because they had been willing to sacrifice their lives for it, David refused to drink it, and offered it up to the Lord instead.

In the left wing Saint Joseph sits at a distance with his back to the scene, and warms some swaddling clothes by the fire. He is elderly, and his age helps support the orthodox belief in Mary's perpetual virginity. The ruins around him signify the passing of the old order and the dawn of a new age. Saint Peter holding the Keys of the Kingdom presents the male donor of the painting, who is reverently kneeling. On the opposite wing the female donor kneels alongside her patron, Saint Agnes. Both donors have their coats of arms represented, like calling cards at an exposition.

In the far distance one can see Jerusalem with its elaborate towers (and even a windmill!). But between the cityscape and the stable, the seemingly tranquil pastoral scene contains disturbing signs that all is not well. In the middle ground on either side of the central panel, two opposing armies race toward each other as if they were about to engage in war. In the left panel, beyond the ruins, a number of revelers dance mindlessly to the tune of a bagpipe, unconscious of the armed conflict about to commence. In the middle ground of the right panel, wolves prey on humans to devour their flesh. One wonders whether the curious shepherds who comically peer in and around the stable are paying any attention to their endangered flock. And, most curious of all, the half-naked and eerie figure stepping through the door of the stable adorned with bizarre jewelry and accompanied by a daunting retinue looks very dangerous indeed! Who is he? Scholars have differing opinions. Could he be the Antichrist? He wears a turban camouflaged by a crown of thorns and wears a red cloak that would mimic Jesus in his Passion. Could he be King Herod, who has secretly followed the Wise Men to their destination? Is he a Kabbalistic image of Adam redeemed by the coming of the Second Adam? Is he an allegorical figure of Heresy, a phenomenon that has plagued the Church from the beginning of its existence, like a wolf ever waiting to attack its prey? Whatever his significance, one thing is certain in the world that Bosch represents: Evil has not been banished from the earth by the birth of its Savior. It continues to plague human existence.

But like the star that shines high in the sky and drew these Magi from distant lands, Hope has entered the world in the form of an Infant. Sitting on a bright corporal-white napkin on the altar of Mary's body adorned in midnight blue robes, he commands the veneration of the wise. Faith sees in his frail form the Master of all creation. And Love will be the message that can transform this ominous vale of tears into a new Paradise.

THE ADORATION
OF THE MAGI

The Adoration of the Magi (the *Washington tondo*)
(c. 1440–60),
Fra Angelico (c. 1400–1455) and Fra Filippo Lippi
(c. 1406–1469),
tempera on panel, 54 in.

This work of art is one of the earliest surviving European round paintings. It is also one of the most mysterious. Its richly colored iconography recalls the fairy-tale quality of Medieval paintings. On the other hand, there is also evidence here of a closer study of nature, a scientific rendering more typical of the Renaissance. The date of the painting has been much disputed. Likewise its authorship has been debated. We know that Fra Filippo Lippi, a Carmelite, worked on it at intervals for many years. But another hand can be seen here, perhaps that of Fra Angelico, a Dominican. The two painter monks had different temperaments. Fra Angelico was known for his ethereal representation of angels and holy personages. Fra Filippo Lippi's art was more sensual. It could be said that the tondo painting combines qualities that are both heavenly and earthly, locked together in a close relationship that is wondrously detailed.

The center of the painting focuses on the humble stable and the manger that served as the Christ Child's first bed. The ox reclines beside it while the donkey feeds from it. But this stable has now become a resting place for a number of horses as well. In fact, the painting includes no fewer than seven such beasts, whose foreshortened rear ends boast of the Renaissance dexterity for the art of perspective. Other animals adorn the stable, encoded with a Christological significance. Most notably appears the peacock, whose celestial feathers dramatically drape the humble wooden lintel. It was thought by Medieval man that the flesh of the peacock did not decay. Therefore the bird became a symbol of eternity and resurrection, with its feathers

I n sacred geometry the circle is a highly celebrated shape. It is a symbol of eternity because it has no beginning or end. It is a symbol of birth and fecundity because of its womblike shape. It is also an ancient symbol of the macrocosm and the entirety of creation. For all these symbolic reasons, the *Adoration of the Magi* (also known as the *Washington Tondo*) by Fra Filippo Lippi takes on a totemic presence as three Magi, representing the faithful from all over the world, come to venerate the Birth of Christ.

often imitated in the depiction of angels' wings. The nearby pheasants, too, are representative of a sublime idea. It was thought that these birds took special care to safeguard their young. Because Christ was born to save mankind, so the pheasant took its place in the beastiary of Christ as a symbol of redemption.

The tondo exhibits a colorful array of people parading toward the seated Virgin and Child, as if all mankind were marching behind the three Magi to pay him homage. This reflects what was found in the Offertory chant (drawn from Psalm 72) for the feast of the Epiphany:

> May the kings of Tarshish and the islands
> bring tribute,
> the kings of Arabia and Seba offer gifts.
> May all kings bow before him,
> all nations serve him.
> For he rescues the poor when they cry out,
> the oppressed who have no one to help.
> He shows pity to the needy and the poor
> And saves the lives of the poor.

Poor men in tattered clothing stand and kneel behind the Holy Family while the elegantly vested sages genuflect immediately before them. Here the depiction of the three Magi reflects the three ages of man: youth, maturity, and old age. The eldest one leads the others, and with his heavily bearded head bowed, he lifts the Infant's foot in order to kiss it. The seated Madonna supports the baby Jesus on her lap and looks down upon this humble gesture with serene repose while Saint Joseph, standing beside her, raises his hand in approval.

A crescent moon of foliage decorates the bottom half of the tondo. The bright array of flowers and clover creates a carpet of honor for the noble visitors, and at the same time they point to the glory of

the Resurrection. In contrast, the singular cypress tree near the gateway takes on a funereal interpretation. All are called to pass from death to eternal life in Christ Jesus. The old order is passing away, just as the ruins of King David's palace in the background signify. Atop those ruins stand semi-nude figures draped in baptismal white. The sacrament of initiation, a ceremony in which the catechumens were divested of their garments, submerged in water, and clothed in white, was commemorated in past ages on the feast of the Epiphany. But these Renaissance nudes can also allude to the spirits that rose from the tombs and wandered into the city of Jerusalem after the earth shook to its very core and Christ's supreme sacrifice was accomplished (Mt 27:51-53).

A medley of symbols signifying life, death, and resurrection permeate the tondo with seemingly inexhaustible modes of interpretation. Even a Marian gloss can be drawn from this painting, starting with the archway that recalls in the litany the Virgin's title "Gate of Heaven." The Madonna, who is seated on a rock, cushions the Christ Child in her lap. She is intimately connected to him, for her stone throne can in turn be interpreted as the cornerstone of salvation, Christ himself. All around her, as signs of decay and new life appear, the prophecy of Simeon comes to mind (Lk 2:34-35):

> *Behold, this child is destined for the fall and rise of many in Israel, and to be a sign that will be contradicted...so that the thoughts of many hearts may be revealed.*

THE HOLY KINSHIP

The Holy Kinship (1470),
Westphalian School,
27.2 x 56.7 in., Saint Servatius Cathedral Treasury,
Maastricht, The Netherlands

The "Holy Family" in Christian iconography means that nuclear family that was Jesus, Mary, and Joseph. By contrast, the "Holy Kinship" refers to the extended family of Jesus and his many relatives through the bloodline of Saint Anne, the Mother of the Virgin Mary. Saint Jerome in his translation of Scripture believed that, when certain persons were referred to as *brothers* of Jesus, the Hebrew word could connote cousins and those who were close in bloodline but different in parentage. By the 12th century certain theologians in the west tried to understand better Saint Anne, the grandmother of Jesus, and her special role in sacred history. It was also in that century that theologian Peter Lombard, in his phrase-by-phrase commentary on Saint Paul's Epistle to the Galatians, grappled with the problematic reference to the Apostle James as the *brother of the Lord* (1:19), and conjectured that he could either be the offspring of Saint Joseph by a previous marriage or a descendent of Saint Anne, whom some believed had been married three times. Those who gave credence to the latter embraced what has been called the *trinubium*, the belief that Saint Anne had three daughters, all named Mary, by three different husbands, thus making her not only the grandmother of Jesus but also the grandmother of five of the twelve apostles: John the Evangelist, James the Greater, James the Less, Simon, and Jude.

In the late 15th and early 16th centuries the notion of the Holy Kinship of Christ became extremely popular in Germany and the Low

Countries, and this Westphalian painting represents the extended family of Jesus as if its members were gathered for a reunion and ready to celebrate a mystical picnic on a grassy knoll. The background is gold, signifying that they inhabit sacred time and space. Anne is seated in the center, on the highest register of the knoll, with an open book in her hand. She is talking to her first husband Joachim, father of the Virgin Mary. He holds a small scroll while pointing to a book lying between them on the bank. Anne's second husband Cleophas is seated on Joachim's right, while Anne's third husband Salomas is placed on her left. Cleophas and Salomas are both holding scrolls, which are symbolically associated with the Old Testament, whereas the bound book represents the New Testament. As grandparents of Christ, Joachim and Anne bridge both Testaments, and the bound book is significantly placed directly above the small figure of Christ standing on Mary's lap in the second register. Here the Word of God is symbolically aligned with the Word made flesh.

In the second register below them, their daughter Mary is positioned in the center of the painting. In tribute to her perpetual virginity, Mary's hair flows freely like that of a maiden. Unlike the other matrons in the painting, she wears no veil. The Christ Child is dressed in a knee-length white tunic, the color of purity and innocence. His head is turned towards his adopted father Joseph, who is depicted as an elderly man, in stark contrast to his much-younger wife. This age difference is purposeful, for its aim was to support Mary's virginity.

On Joseph's left sits Saint Anne's second daughter, Mary Cleophas, nursing her youngest infant. Two more sons sit at her feet. They are Simon the Zealot, who holds an inkwell, and Jude Thaddeus, who is writing a letter. A fourth son, James the Lesser, squirms in the lap of his father Alphaeus while ignoring the spectacles he has been given to play with. A well-studied understanding of the restless animation of children can be seen in this painting alongside a symbolic integration of objects connecting them to biblical tradition. Both James the Less and Jude Thaddeus have written material sprawled across their infant bodies because in later years, as mature apostles, they would be credited as authors of letters contained in the canon of Scripture.

To the right of the Virgin Mary sits Saint Anne's third daughter, Mary Salome. Her husband Zebedee is behind her, holding a pair of spectacles in order to read a sheet of paper. Mary Salome's son, James the Greater, finds a hiding place beneath his mother's blue cloak, while his naked little brother, John the Evangelist, sits on her lap. Elizabeth, Mary's elderly cousin, offers little John an apple. Her own son, John the Baptist, is standing beneath her, dressed uncharacteristically in a smart little tunic and hat. Presaging his fate, the ensemble is painted entirely in red, the color of martyrdom. Elizabeth's husband Zechariah sits in profile above them. With an unfurled scroll he talks about Old Testament prophecy with Saint Anne's third husband, Salomas. Balancing this construct on the far left of the painting sits Emyu in profile. He was reputedly the grandson of Saint Anne's sister. His wife and child are seated below him, and it is through his line that the first bishop of Maastricht, Saint Servatius, traced his genealogy. The painting is in the church dedicated to that saint, and it invites the worshipers of that town spiritually to join these illustrious relatives of Jesus as if they were part of the family, too, bonded by faith.

Unlike *The Tree of Jesse* and other artistic representations of Christ's lineage, *The Holy Kinship* tries to penetrate the mysteries of Scripture while emphasizing the female ancestors of Christ and the sublime role of motherhood.

THE PRESENTATION OF JESUS IN THE TEMPLE

The Presentation of Jesus in the Temple (1440–41), Fra Angelico (c. 1400–1455), fresco, 67.3 x 45.6 in., Convent of San Marco, cellule 10, Florence, Italy

Many adjectives have been used to describe the art of Fra Angelico. His work has been called graceful, sweet, and calm, combining the perfect balance between grandeur and restraint. The 19th-century art theorist John Ruskin lionized him as more than just an artist, for he saw exemplified in the friar's work the sublime purity of a saint.

While living at the Dominican house of San Marco in Florence, Fra Angelico painted in each friar's cell a scene drawn from Scripture and Tradition, a pictorial representation that would inspire the occupant to pray in the manner of the Order's founder, Saint Dominic. The frescoes are an eloquent expression of the Order's spirituality, a testament to the potent blending of image and prayer.

In each tableau a feast of the liturgical calendar was pictured, including witnesses drawn primarily from the various saints of the Order. These witnesses would strike a pose derived from a popular Dominican prayer manual, showing some of the nine symbolic postures assumed by Saint Dominic and later handed down to the men and women of the Order.

The Presentation of Jesus in the Temple was the scene painted by Fra Angelico for the double cell of the prior, or superior of the house. At the time of the painting, Saint Antoninus of Florence, a fatherly figure who would later become the beloved bishop of the city, occupied this room. As prior he had to safeguard the law and traditions of the Order and pray for the brethren, especially the young friars and novices of the house. The theme chosen for his cell was not coincidental, since the Feast of the Presentation of Jesus had long been observed by Dominicans as the day on which to commemorate the dedication of young religious to the Order. The feast was celebrated with a candlelight procession in the cloister. This in itself was symbolic, for the theme of light is intimately connected to the feast, both scripturally and liturgically.

In the Gospel of Luke (2:22-40) we read that Mary and Joseph took Jesus to the Temple in Jerusalem forty days after his birth in order to perform the ritual redemption of their firstborn as required by law (Ex 13:12-15) and to complete the purification of the mother after childbirth, which demanded that a lamb be sacrificed—or, if one were poor, then two turtledoves would suffice (Lv 12). Upon entering the Temple they encountered a righteous old

man named Simeon, to whom it had been promised by the Holy Spirit that he would not taste death until he had seen the Messiah. Drawn immediately to the Child, he took Jesus in his arms and uttered the canticle thereafter known in Latin as the *Nunc dimittis*, a prayer recited by the friars in their service of compline just before retiring to sleep:

> Now, Master, you may let your servant
> go in peace,
> according to your word,
> for my eyes have seen your salvation, which
> you have prepared in sight of all the peoples,
> a light for revelation to the Gentiles,
> and glory for your people Israel.
> (Lk 2:29-32)

The prophetess Anna was also in the temple. She was an aged widow from the tribe of Asher. She gave thanks to God and spoke of the Child to all who were awaiting the redemption of Jerusalem (Lk 2:36-38).

Because Simeon referred to the Christ Child as "light" this feast was nicknamed Candlemas (Candle Mass) when, traditionally, candles used in the church and at home were blessed and distributed. So, too, in the Dominican tradition the candle processions and the dedication of the young in the priory made the account found in Scripture reverberate through monastic time in liturgy and symbol.

Fra Angelico's fresco of the Presentation is filled with cheerful if muted color, but the dazzling white of the Christ Child's swaddling

clothes pull one's attention to Jesus as if in a spotlight. Fra Angelico's art is Christocentric, and while the limpid gestures of his figures may lack the drama and emotionalism found in the work of Giotto, who perfectly exemplified Franciscan spirituality, the art of San Marco focuses on the subtler and more abstract ideas that became a wellspring for Dominican preaching. Scripture, tradition, the *Golden Legend*, and spiritual treatises all fed into Fra Angelico's work. Drawing on such sources, the friar could contemplate the sublime reason why Jesus allowed himself to be born poor, and submitted himself to the laws of sinful

time. The black-robed woman also acts as fore-shadowing of Mary as the grieving mother, for at this ceremony Simeon also predicted that a sword was destined to pierce Mary, thus giving rise to her popular image as the Mater Dolorosa. The other witness is the Dominican martyr Saint Peter of Verona. Both witnesses imitate the hand gestures and genuflections of Saint Dominic's fourth mode of prayer, invoked especially when praying for the young.

The kneeling Peter provides an interesting postscript to this painting. A flow of blood trickles down his skull. An assassin for hire named Carino murdered him in 1252. Ambushing Peter as he walked along a country road, Carino split his skull open with an axe. In Peter's agony he began to recite the Apostles Creed before Carino plunged a dagger into his chest. The nobility of the saint's martyrdom caused Carino to repent of his crime, enter the Order as a lay brother, live a holy life, and later be declared a blessed.

Blood can transform souls. So can paint. And shining behind both of these human achievements is God's wondrous grace.

men, how he would expiate through suffering and redeem the world through the sacrificial and obediential love with which he humbled himself even to the rituals of the Law.

Fra Angelico has composed the scene as if they were actors on a bare stage. Joseph holds the turtledoves; Mary hands the Infant to Simeon before the altar of sacrifice. And while the woman dressed in black is meant to represent the prophetess Anna, she may have a double identity as a Dominican witness, possibly Blessed Villana de Bottia, whose cult was popular in Florence at that

THE TRIUMPH OF THE INNOCENTS

The Triumph of the Innocents (c. 1883–84), William Holman Hunt (1827–1910), oil on canvas, 61.4 x 100 in.

" In this English picture all the story of the escape, as of the flight, is told in fullness of peace and yet of compassion. The travel is in the dead of night; the way unseen and unknown; but, partly stooping from the starlight, and partly floating on the desert mirage, move with the Holy Family the glorified souls of the Innocents. Clear in celestial light and gathered into child-garlands of gladness, they look to the Child in whom they live, and yet for whom they die. Waters of the River of Life flow before on the sands; the Christ stretches out his arms to the nearest of them—leaning from his mother's breast."

This enthusiastic description of William Holman Hunt's painting *The Triumph of the Innocents* was made by the influential 19th-century art critic and theorist John Ruskin, who declared the work "the greatest religious painting of our time." Hunt was one of the founders of the Pre-Raphaelite Brotherhood, a clique of young, idealistic Victorian painters who sought to depict truth through a close observation of nature. Their scientific accuracy did not, however, preclude explorations of themes with a devout religious content. Strikingly original in its conception, Hunt's canvas pulls together the themes of death and resurrection and juxtaposes them within the scene of the Holy Family's celebrated flight into Egypt. In a salute to those innocent children whose lives were sacrificed in the massacre wrought by a jealous and vengeful King Herod following the wonder of the Nativity and the glory of the Epiphany in Bethlehem, Hunt eulogizes in paint those infants whose martyrdom the Church has liturgically commemorated during Christmastide ever since the 5th century.

Here among the clusters of children, one can see babes floating in air and stretching as they awake to the afterlife. One child peers down and curiously examines his ripped garment, torn by the blade of the sword that killed him. Another group of children, festooned with garlands, interlock their hands and arms as they cross the celestial stream of Living Water, a baptismal reference to which they are connected by the blood they have shed. Bubbles rising from the watery pools contribute to the ethereal quality of the painting, and in one of the airy globes, Hunt has painted a biblical allegory symbolizing the Jewish millennium. As the earthly and heavenly party moves forward, the Virgin Mary's eyes connect with the viewer and a gracious smile curls her lips. She is the one figure who invites us to enter into the wonders of this painting. A young and muscular Saint Joseph, on the other hand, cautiously turns his back toward us. Bearing over his shoulders some of the few possessions he could salvage in their hasty departure, he seems to be surveying the landscape for any sign of approaching danger.

It was a difficult work to execute, admitted the artist, who painted several versions of the painting during his long and illustrious career. "With such a chain of entwined children in positions impossible for babies to keep, the work demanded intense perseverance and study," Hunt declared. Another of the challenges he had to face was the problem of light for a scene that takes place in the dark of night. He at first intended to portray the figures under the silvery veil of moonlight, but then he changed his mind: "When the large work expanded before me I judged that in the pearly hue of the moon alone, a picture of such dimensions would be monotonous in aspect, and that a supernatural light on the ghostly infants would help to convey the impression of their celestial nature." In order to test the quality of light, Hunt viewed the countryside around Jerusalem through an ocular lens on a bright night. To his surprise, the focus revealed the scene not in silvery tones, but in the warmer tones found in daylight. This he adopted in his painting in the depiction of the Innocents, who are also outlined and haloed with a radiant aura.

While Ruskin lavished praise on the painting, some critics were disturbed by the artist's all-too-easy blending of the supernatural with the natural. The painting renders itself as a vision, one in which the Christ Child alone seems fully to see and understand as he extends his arm, bearing shafts of wheat to the celestial babes beside him. Fellow Pre-Raphaelite painter Frederick George Stevens criticized the work for its "strange mixture of real and unreal," and he declared it "self-contradictory and puzzling." Likewise, critics of the 20th century have attacked the work for its bold religiosity, its sentimentality, and its masculine and European perspective of a Middle Eastern scene. But Hunt, a devout and committed Christian, would find no problem in blending natural with supernatural truth. The biased categories of the Enlightenment, separating the spiritual from the physical and reducing religion to a species of superstition, found no harbor in the artist's work. Rather he conceives and looks at this scene through the eyes of faith and with the wonder of a child.

It is a fitting perspective to take for a scene that would otherwise engender panic and fear. It is a message of hope and peace in a time of great adversity.

REST ON THE FLIGHT INTO EGYPT

Rest on the Flight into Egypt (1805–06), Philipp Otto Runge (1777–1810), oil on canvas, 38.5 x 51.9 in.

Sometimes a flower means more than just a flower and a tree represents more than a tree. When nature dons the mantle of symbolism, a whole new set of meanings emerges.

The German Romantic painters of the 19th century enthusiastically imbued nature with mystical symbolism, and one of its greatest proponents was the young artist Philip Otto Runge (1777–1810). Combining classical motifs and Christian iconography with a renewed sense of the mythology of landscape, Runge's new art exemplified the Romantic quest to make contact with the Absolute, with God, in meditative interpretations of nature. He believed in the underlying unity of all creation with the divine. He also believed that humans could see themselves, their virtues, and their passions, in plants and all natural phenomena. Thus, when Runge painted a tree or a lily it would often take on the importance of a totem. His depictions of flowers and children were often flamboyantly exaggerated as they assumed symbolic poses. Light and color were also heightened, opening the door to his mystical interpretation of ordinary finite things.

Here in his *Rest on the Flight into Egypt*, the artist takes a traditional biblical episode and infuses the landscape with a fortified awareness of the divine. The Holy Family is seen reposing in the foreground with a vast stretch of the Egyptian countryside displayed in the distance. The Nile has flooded its banks, and a lone pyramid can be seen beyond the raised hand of the Child Jesus. The pyramids were already regarded as ancient when the Holy Family fled to Egypt. They were monuments of the old order now crumbling from the weight of time. The flooding Nile that fertilized the soil of Egypt and caused new life to grow every year becomes now a metaphor for Baptism. The pyramid is a symbol of death, built to receive a pharaoh's mummy. The old order is indeed passing away, for the light that surrealistically infuses the painting with a mystical radiance is the light of daybreak. Christ, the Light of the World, brings new hope into the darkness of a world enslaved.

The bearded and bald-headed figure of Saint Joseph sits in repose. The Holy Family is now safe. King Herod's murderous wrath does not extend into this foreign land. Yet Christ's sacrifice to come is hinted at in the figure of the beast of burden. Joseph's donkey grazes on thistle leaves, symbolic of the gall offered to Christ at the crucifixion. Joseph's staff is pointed in such a way as visually to connect the donkey with the Christ Child, who gazes up in rapture at the blossoming tree that hovers over him and the Virgin Mary like a large floral umbrella. Runge loved to paint children, and

saw infancy as the special conduit of nature's vital forces, the stage of human development that defied the rationality of an organized adult world and embraced the wondrous and the miraculous without shame. The artist's declaration that "we must become children again if we wish to achieve the best" parallels Christ's own teachings and underscores the very essence of Romantic yearning. Children were seen as an unspoiled life force in the mystery of nature. It is no coincidence that the cultural milieu that produced Schiller, Novalis, and Wordsworth also saw a rebirth in children's fairy tales with the writings of Jacob and Wilhelm Grimm and Hans Christian Anderson.

There is no more wondrous child than the Infant Jesus, and Runge portrays him stretched out upon the ground and enveloped in Mary's protective veil. The Virgin's sweetly modulated face with eyes devoted only to him gives evidence to a mother's care, while her clasped hands seem to betray a nervousness that she might still harbor, for they have not yet settled in this strange land.

By contrast, the carefree Child Jesus is the lone visionary in this composition, for the artist has him communicating with the cherub nestled under the tree's flowered canopy. The tree is thought to look like a Christmas Rose Tree, but it is really like no other tree found on earth. Could it be suggestive of the Tree of Life, which had been barred to Adam and Eve in Eden? Just as the cross of Christ has been likened to that tree, so too does the symbolism of redemption permeate this angel-infested arbor. One cherub perched on top plays a harp while greeting the dawn of a new day. And the cherub communicating with Christ hands the divine Child a lily, symbol of purity and resurrection.

While the Holy Family fled the bloodbath of Herod's massacre of the innocents, Runge and his art were reacting to the apocalyptic terror of the French Revolution. In this unfinished painting he poured out his Romantic hopes, searching for Innocence regained and Paradise mystically renewed.

THE VIRGIN OF THE LILIES

The Virgin of the Lilies (1899),
Carlos Schwabe (1866–1926),
pencil and watercolor, 38.2 x 18.5 in.

From an ancient Greek myth the story was told that when Zeus, king of the gods, had sired Hercules with a mortal woman, he placed the infant at the breast of Hera, his wife and queen of the gods, while she was sleeping. Upon awakening and seeing that she had involuntarily been nursing a child that was not her own, she flung young Hercules away from her, and the nourishing liquid flowing from her breast created the Milky Way.

That which did not remain in the heavens fell to earth and formed lilies, a flower that has long been associated with fruitfulness and divine blessings.

Christianity appropriated the lily and developed its symbolism beyond that of the Greeks' own queen of heaven. Over and above the ancients, Mary's role as the nursing Mother of the Son of God has long been revered in Christian art and culture, giving her the title of "Madonna Lactans." On the road leading out of Bethlehem stands today the ancient Milk Grotto, a shrine venerated for nearly 2,000 years. Legend has it that Mary stopped there on the flight into Egypt to nurse the Christ Child inside the safety of its cave. The whiteness of the limestone is associated with Mary's role as a nursing mother, and women from all over the world have made pilgrimages there asking the Madonna to help them in their pregnancies. But the lily, that celestial white flower with its earlier symbolism rooted in pagan fecundity and nourishment, evolved through Christianity into a sign of purity that pointed to the even more sublime mystery of the Incarnation: How did Mary conceive her divine Child and give birth to him while still remaining a virgin? This paradox is celebrated in scenes of the Annunciation where the Archangel Gabriel appears to Mary, bringing her a lily. The fleur-de-lis, with its three petals united by a single stem, has embedded in its emblematic symbolism Mary's own supernatural relationship to the Holy Trinity: Mary being the daughter of the Father, the Mother of the Son, and the bride of the Holy Spirit.

Carlos Schwabe was baptized a Protestant in his native Germany and raised in Geneva, Switzerland. In time he progressed from his original occupation as a wallpaper designer and illustrator to delve into the world of Symbolism, a period of artistic ferment at the fin-de-siècle when religious and emotional impulses sought meaning within the mystic blend of symbols, old and new. He settled in France, one of the great centers of this movement, and adapted easily to the Catholic iconography that permeated it. Enjoying the patronage of a French countess and

using his wife (coincidentally named Maria) as his model, the artist created a number of images of the Virgin Mary in mystical environments. He considered his *Virgin of the Lilies* of 1899 the greatest achievement of his career up to that point.

In this composition, Schwabe has placed the Virgin and Child on a cloud far above the earth. The vantage point of the viewer, looking down from the heavens over hills and valleys, over a meandering river around which towns have nestled, is something we take for granted today in the age of the airplane. But Schwabe's painting was executed before airplanes and dirigibles were invented. His inspiration came instead from the experimental work of the French photographer Nadar, who carried his camera up into hot-air balloons, giving viewers a picture of the earth that had heretofore been reserved for divinity.

The sinewy bright clouds create an ethereal platform that contrasts sharply with the dark pigments of the terra firma below. The Virgin and Child walk down a lily-lined path, symbolizing the stairway to Paradise. The tall, rigid stems of the lilies act as organic balusters, culminating in the coping of the flowers in full bloom. The artist was pleased with the way that he had incorporated so many shades of white and blue into the composition, colors that are most often associated with the Virgin Mary. The haloes of Mother and Child unite to create a moonlike radiance over the earth. It is within that combined radiance that one can see

the Christ Child holding in his hands three small objects, pressing them against his lips. They are nails, instruments of the passion, splayed in such a way as to look like a fleur-de-lis. This brings the lily to its highest symbolic development in the iconography of Christian art. For the flower is not only a symbol of motherhood, purity, and virginity, but also a symbol of the Resurrection. The whiteness of the flower recalls the shroud that enveloped Christ's body in the tomb, while its horn-shaped petals represent the heralding of the Good News that Christ has risen, the firstborn from the dead.

Nature and mysticism are here united. The color and contours of this elegant flower bid us to contemplate its beauty and to see within it the reflection of the Creator's divine plan.

OUR LADY WITH THE INFANT JESUS RIDING ON A LAMB WITH SAINT JOHN

Our Lady with the Infant Jesus Riding on a Lamb with Saint John (1800), William Blake (1757–1827), pen and tempera on canvas, 10.7 x 15.2 in.

In his book of poems *Songs of Innocence and Experience* (1789), the visionary Protestant artist William Blake contrasted childhood and the innocence of nature with an industrialized adult world that he viewed as mechanized, corrupt, and cruel. One particular poem of the collection, *The Lamb*, was presented in the voice of a child looking at the little animal, and asking it those guileless, metaphysical questions children often pose:

> Little Lamb, who made thee?
> Dost thou know who made thee?
> Gave thee life, and bid thee feed,
> By the stream and o'er the mead;
> Gave thee clothing of delight,
> Softest clothing wooly bright;
> Gave thee such a tender voice,
> Making all the vales rejoice?
> Little Lamb, who made thee?
> Dost thou know who made thee?

The singsong quality of this descriptive stanza renders lyrical support to the amazement and curiosity a child might feel when first placed in a pastoral setting. Yet Blake completes the poem with another stanza that answers all these innocent questions with a spiritual maturity grounded in the child's satisfied wonder, something that supersedes by faith and the power of symbol the mere scientific observation of the scene:

> Little Lamb, I'll tell thee,
> Little Lamb, I'll tell thee.
> He is called by thy name,
> For he calls himself a Lamb.
> He is meek, and he is mild;
> He became a little child.
> I a child, and thou a lamb,
> We are called by his name.
> Little Lamb, God bless thee!
> Little Lamb, God bless thee!

This riddle of an answer that ends in a benediction completes the poem. The lamb was created by the one "who calls himself a Lamb," and identifies with the child. Both lamb and child, symbols of innocence and meekness, are linked to Christ in Scripture, and therefore it is not surprising that eleven years later Blake depicted the Christ Child riding on a lamb in one of his painted illustrations for the Bible. It is not a literal depiction of a scene from the Bible, but rather a poetic scene distilled from various elements found in Holy Writ.

Christ called himself the *Good Shepherd* (Jn 10:11), watching over his flock and guiding them through the narrow sheep gate. Yet elsewhere in Scripture Christ is himself paradoxically

identified with the meekest and humblest of the flock, portrayed as a lamb. John the Baptist pointed to Christ as *the Lamb of God, who takes away the sin of the world* (Jn 1:29). It was to shepherds in a field that angels first announced his Nativity (Lk 2:8-14). Like the lambs sacrificed in the Temple, Jesus himself would be offered up on the cross as a redemptive sacrifice to the Father. And in the Book of Revelation, it is Christ in the guise of the Mystic Lamb who is worshiped and adored (Rv 5:6-14). Christ is Shepherd and lamb, God and man. His solicitude for children, and his identification with the small and the meek, prompts him to tell his disciples that *unless they become like little children, they will not enter the kingdom of heaven* (cf. Mt 18:2-5).

Gathering all of these concepts together, Blake's depiction of the Christ Child riding on a lamb is a simple artistic representation of several complex theological ideas. The scene is set in an idyllic landscape tinted in tones of green and gold. The living waters of a winding stream bring life to the valley. John the Baptist and Christ are portrayed as children. They are depicted nude to accentuate the notion of youthful innocence. Just as John was the herald for Christ in Scripture, so he leads his cousin on foot while carrying shafts of wheat and the coiling vine of the grape, both Eucharistic symbols. The Christ Child has his arms outstretched as he rides the lamb. His little body strikes a cruciform pose. One limb points forward to a future destined for sacrifice, while the other rests on the Virgin's arm for support. She is intimately connected to her Son in his trials and in his triumphs. Elegantly coiffed and wearing a long, flowing gown, she is attentive to his every move. She is

devoted and protective as he boldly moves forward without holding on. The figures are lined up as if in procession, a foreshadowing of his entry into Jerusalem, when, as a hero in his prime, he will ride on the back of another beast, a donkey, the traditional symbol of the Hebrews, who on that day would flood the streets, cover them with palm branches, and call him the king of Israel.

But moments of triumph, peace, and goodness cannot erase the fact that evil and death also exist and taint creation. Blake wrote other poems to contemplate this paradox. But here in his paradise garden of purity and joy, where motherly attention drives all cares away, the celebration of new life and innocence is illustrated, and the shimmering dawn of happiness breaks forth to envelop the world.

THE CARPENTER'S SHOP (Christ in the Home of His Parents)

The Carpenter's Shop (Christ in the Home of His Parents) (1849–50),
Sir John Everett Millais (1829–1896), oil on canvas, 34 x 55.1 in.

The picture takes us into a carpenter's shop, where an accident has just occurred. A little boy has tried to help his father, but in doing so he has injured the palm of his hand on a nail sticking out of the board of wood. Blood oozes forth and splashes onto his foot. The father gently looks at the wound while the mother kneels down and offers the boy consolation and extends her cheek for a kiss. The other workers in the room pause and gaze upon the wounded child with momentary concern.

This Victorian painting received a hailstorm of criticism when it was exhibited in London over 160 years ago. The artist, a member of the Pre-Raphaelite Brotherhood that sought to re-invigorate Christian art, wanted to portray an everyday scene in the life of the Holy Family and imbue it with symbolic significance. But English critics were wary of artistic brotherhoods, fearing that they smacked of Roman Catholicism, and they deplored the mundane manner in which the sacred characters were depicted. Even Charles Dickens railed against it, calling the wounded child a

"wry-necked, blubbering boy in a nightgown," and his mother "so horrible in her ugliness" that she belonged "in the lowest gin-shop in England." The work became so controversial that Queen Victoria had the painting removed from exhibition and sent to the palace for a private viewing.

Victorian eyes were used to seeing their religious figures exalted. But this artist wanted to show the dirt, the grime, and the accidents that are part of everyday working life. With a documentarian's approach he meticulously recreated a 19th-century carpenter's shop and projected it back in time to Nazareth, where Saint Joseph is aided in his work by Mary, Jesus, and an extended family that includes Saint Anne and John the Baptist. The figures in the painting look ordinary, but the symbolism behind the details imbue the picture with a profound spiritual significance.

It only takes eyes to see.

The wound in the palm of the Christ Child foreshadows the wounds he will receive at his Crucifixion in both his hands and feet. Above his head hang tools that will also play a part in his Passion: a hammer, a ladder, pliers, and nails. The triangular set-square hanging in the background suggests the heavenly Trinity of Father, Son, and Holy Spirit while the earthly trinity of Mary, Jesus, and Joseph are linked together in this moment of pain and love. Mary extends her cheek to console the wounded Child, just as she would later station herself near to his cross to share in his pain and sorrow. Her

furrowed brow reveals the empathy she feels for her Child, who is suffering and in need of comfort. Saint John fittingly carries over a bowl of water to bathe the wound. The water and his animal skin loincloth are attributes that will forever identify him as the Baptizer. A further baptismal association can be made here with the white dove perched on the ladder over the head of Jesus, a foreshadowing of the Holy Spirit that will one day appear over the mature Christ at the river Jordan.

The lumber behind John reminds the viewer of the planks of the cross. Likewise, the carpenter's table and the door on which the Holy Family is working take on a sacramental significance when merged with the blood of Christ. At the table of the Last Supper Christ would institute the Holy Eucharist, thereby opening the door to everlasting life. By his blood we are redeemed. The shedding of his blood is forever commemorated on the altar of sacrifice.

The protruding sticks of the unfinished wicker basket on the left of the painting are a reference to the Flagellation. And the sheep pressing against the sheepfold in the background behind the stooping attendant signify the Christian flock yearning for their Good Shepherd.

These salvific symbols are scattered and encoded throughout the painting with the casualness of the wood shavings that litter the floor. On the surface, every detail seems terribly mundane—even

to the dirt caught beneath the laboring Joseph's fingernails. But in life, as in art, one must rise above the ordinary to perceive a higher vision.

And this is done with the eyes of faith.

THE HEAVENLY AND EARTHLY TRINITIES

The Heavenly and Earthly Trinities (1690–1710), Circle of Diego Quispe Tito, School of Cuzco, Peru, oil on canvas, 74 x 47 in.

An array of brightly decorated images fills the canvas. In the upper register, an older, bearded figure floats in the clouds. He is supported by angels. This is God the Father, the Creator, the Ancient of Days, with a triangular halo symbolic of the Trinity. Indeed, the entire canvas is a Trinitarian meditation. Vertically, it shows the heavenly Trinity of Father, Holy Spirit, and Incarnate Son intersecting with the "earthly trinity" composed horizontally of the Blessed Virgin Mary, the Christ Child, and Saint Joseph.

In the figure of Jesus the vertical axis of heaven conjoins and unites itself to the horizontal axis of the earth.

The term "earthly trinity" was applied by theologians to Jesus, Mary, and Joseph long before notions of the nuclear family came into vogue. The Holy Family is an icon par excellence of the nuclear family, one that concentrates not on the older notions of an "extended" family (which would include Saints Anne and Joachim, Mary's parents, and an array of cousins which are often referred to as *brothers and sisters* in Scripture),

but rather those who are bound together by a relational identity composed of father, mother, and offspring. After the Council of Trent, images of the earthly trinity became popular throughout Europe and the Americas. Here the earthly trinity is intimately connected to the heavenly Trinity and to the Church, both theologically and symbolically. And in this relationship, Saint Joseph plays an important part.

Saint Joseph holds a lily, the symbol of chastity and a sign of divine election that figures prominently in the apocryphal accounts of his betrothal to Mary. In their virginal union, Mary and Joseph are rendered angelic, a return to the life lived in Eden. St. Jerome equated virginity with paradise. "Eve was a virgin in Paradise," he wrote "After the garment of skins her married life began." Here, the notion of the Holy Family as the restoration of Paradise on earth is further supported by the glorification of clothing, rendered in the decorative golden *brocateado* of the Peruvian painter. The Virgin Mother's cloak is studded with stars, evocative of her heavenly crown in the Book of Revelation. And the clothing of Jesus and Joseph is embellished with golden flowers, like that of God the Father. Mary, the New Eve, holds Christ's hand. Their flesh is appropriately joined, since she bore him in her womb by the power of the Holy Spirit, represented above by the dove. Saint Joseph's palm is open and extended over the hand of Jesus, which clutches a pilgrim's staff. In the Christ Child's early journey through life,

Joseph stands guard over him as protector and foster father. Joseph's authority as vicar and patriarch is derived from God the Father, whose own hands above are likewise open and extended.

Unlike so many depictions of Saint Joseph, this one does not portray him as an old man. Scripture nowhere indicates that Joseph was advanced in age. The idea of a decrepit Joseph became popular with certain Fathers of the Church, and lingered through the Middle Ages as a response to heretics who doubted Christ's divine origins and the perpetual virginity of Mary. But this response was bound to backfire: if Joseph were portrayed as a man so old that he would be incapable of fatherhood, then dissenters were equally able to conjecture that Mary must have been an adulteress and Jesus was illegitimate! Reason tells us that Joseph was most probably in the prime of life, for how else could he have engaged in a profession of manual labor, traveled great distances with Mary and Jesus, and served as their protector?

Here Saint Joseph is seen as a handsome and vigorous man leading the Holy Family along a path that is garnished with flowers by angels. In the temporal sphere of history, the Church is the Body of Christ, Mary is its Mother, and Joseph is its Guardian. The rehabilitation of Saint Joseph as a vital figure in the makeup of the Holy Family, emphasizing his active and devoted participation in its concord of love, further bolsters all notions of his sanctity and his exalted vocation as protector of Christ and of the Church.

THE FINDING OF THE SAVIOR IN THE TEMPLE

The Finding of the Savior in the Temple (1854–60),
William Holman Hunt (1827–1910),
oil on canvas, 33.7 x 55.5 in.

Many years before he produced his spectacular painting on the *Triumph of the Innocents*, William Holman Hunt conceived of the idea of creating a work taken from the life of Christ and filling it with archaeological exactitude. He was inspired by the passage in Luke (2:41-50) wherein the boy Jesus slips away from his parents, who were returning to Nazareth, and amazes the doctors and sages in the Temple in Jerusalem with his wisdom and knowledge. Discovering that their Child was missing, Mary and Joseph returned frantically to Jerusalem, where they found the boy engaged with the sages.

When asked why he had caused them so much distress, Jesus simply replied that they should not have worried but should have known that he must be about his Father's business in his Father's house. It is an important event prior to the public ministry of Christ, wherein the adolescent Jesus starts to exert his independence and prepare for the salvific mission ahead.

Hunt traveled all the way to Palestine in order to soak up the local atmosphere and channel it into his painting. No detail escaped his attention. He hired male sitters from among the many destitute Jews living in the city. But events unraveled as a European Jew named Albert Cohn convinced the models to sit for the artist no longer. He placed a curse on Hunt and claimed that the artist was part of an Anglican mission to convert them. He also claimed that the painting would be placed in a church where it would be worshipped, thus causing the models to violate the second commandment. An entire year passed before Hunt could convince the rabbis to lift the ban on Jews posing for him. This discomforting incident caused the artist to depart from the optimism of his scriptural source that had at first inspired him, and it transformed the work into one of confrontation between Christ and the Jewish elders.

Here the artist has portrayed the rabbis of the Temple in a number of unflattering ways, ranging from blindness to pride. Attired to meet the letter of the law rather than its spirit, their clothing is correct, with phylacteries prominently displayed. An old blind rabbi holds the Torah with a boy stationed nearby with a fly whisk, lest any insect defile it. Another boy reverently kisses the cloth that drapes it. A blind beggar sits on the steps leading to the Temple's entrance and this was noted by one critic as an example of "Blind ignorance, sitting outside the Temple…balanced…with a fine study of blind learning within."

In sharp contrast to the stubbornness and blindness of the Jewish elders, one can compare the nobility and affection exhibited by the Holy Family. They stand while the indolent rabbis sit. On the canvas the three figures are shown with an interlocking of their hands and arms, creating a visual torque that is reflected in the halo-like wall decoration behind Joseph's head.

Since Hunt was an Evangelical Christian, he did not reverence Mary in the same way as Catholics do. Yet he and the other Protestant Pre-Raphaelites developed an especially tactile representation of Joseph, who is not afraid to touch the Virgin, even if they did believe in her perpetual virginity. This was a departure from classic Catholic art, where Joseph is seldom seen touching the Virgin. Only the Child Jesus is able to touch his inviolate mother. Here Joseph is represented as a virile figure in his prime with a dark thick beard and ruddy complexion. Garbed in the costume of an observant and righteous Jew, he sports the *payot*, the side locks of a devout Hebrew man. His hand is about to protectively cover the Virgin's hand as she wraps her arm around the shoulders of her Son and presses her face against his. But as she assumes the loving pose of so many icons and paintings from centuries past, one cannot help but feel here that Mary for the first time recognizes a new separation from her Son, whose gaze looks into the future. In his maturity he will have to leave the safety and consolation of her embrace, and, as a mature man, wander throughout the land spreading the Gospel of Salvation until he is delivered into the hands of evil men—like the ones seated before him. Hunt decorated the frame of the painting with Christian symbols that signified the crucifixion of Christ.

Jesus tightens his belt and turns his back on the Jewish elders. The symbolic action of girding one's

loins prefigures his mission of reform. The Scribes and the Pharisees will be the object of his disdain throughout his public ministry. Christ's call for a correction of the abuses inside his Father's house will culminate in his attack on the moneychangers.

The landscape beyond the open door of the Temple reveals the first slopes of Olivet. Death hovers in the background. This is echoed in the cross that Christ wears embroidered on his belt, an ornament that one critic observed was "in common use from time immemorial, being a symbol of life even among the ancient Egyptians." Christ would give new meaning to that ancient symbol, and indeed transform it into a symbol of life everlasting.

THE WEDDING FEAST AT CANA

The Wedding Feast at Cana (c. 1500–1504), Juan de Flandes (active by 1496 and 1519), oil on wood, 8.2 x 6.2 in.

In the Gospel of John (2:1-11) the first public miracle of Jesus is recorded, and the setting is a wedding party that is on the brink of disaster. The event takes place at Cana in Galilee, and Christ and his mother Mary are invited guests. It is discovered that at the height of the festivities the wine has run out, and the bride and groom are about to suffer extreme embarrassment in front of all their guests. Contemporary culture and the media thrive on the crises lurking behind wedding events, and so, too, does this Gospel story have one—yet its problem is filled with theological and even mystical content.

The Church Fathers figured that this wedding took place just a few days after the Baptism of Christ, and after at least some of his disciples had been called to follow him. Mary is mentioned first as having been present at the wedding, and some were of the opinion that perhaps it was one of her relatives who was hosting the affair. That is why she takes command of the situation and why she realizes before others that the wine has run out. Hospitality in the east was seen as a sacred duty, and wine was central to the event. Mary may have seen the dilemma first, but, like any good Jewish mother, she had great confidence in the ability of her Son to solve the problem.

And what was the answer Jesus gave to his mother when she brought the problem to him? He said to her: *Woman, how does your concern affect me? My hour has not yet come.*

Far from being disrespectful, these words do not carry the same weight as they did in the ancient world. Christ calls his mother *Woman* twice in Scripture, once at this wedding feast, and again when he is dying on the cross and gives her over to the care of the Apostle John. In antiquity, "Woman" was a title of respect. In Homer it is what Odysseus called his beloved wife Penelope. And it is the title by which Caesar, the Emperor of Rome, addressed Cleopatra, the famous Queen of Egypt. In any case, Mary did not take her Son's response as an insult. Instead she went straight to the servers of wine and said to them: *Do whatever he tells you.* She may not have known exactly what he would do, but she knew he would do the right thing.

This panel painting is one of forty-seven in a series focused on the lives of Christ and the Virgin Mary. It was painted by the Netherlandish artist Juan de Flandes, who had recently been appointed court painter to Queen Isabella the Catholic of Castile and Leon. Conforming to the queen's taste, the composition is austere, simplified to incorporate the bare number of figures needed for the theme. The round convex mirror in the background was a common motif in Netherlandish paintings at that time.

In the Middle Ages many theologians, Thomas Aquinas included, thought that the bride and groom at the wedding in Cana were none other than John the Evangelist and Mary Magdalene! Thus it follows that John was so enamored by the magnetism of Christ at the wedding that he chose to follow him immediately, thus leaving the poor Magdalene to fall into a spiral of licentious living. The iconography here fits that identification, for the groom is beardless, and he wears a red robe and cloak that was the conventional way of portraying the Beloved Disciple. Furthermore, Queen Isabella's 1505 inventory describes the subject of the painting as a scene from St. John's wedding. It is thought that the artist used as his models Isabella's son, Prince Juan, and his bride Margaret of Austria. They had been married in 1497, a short time after Juan de Flandes' appointment to the court. The figure standing outside in the courtyard at the left of the panel may in fact be a portrait of the artist himself. The scene is set just before the miracle takes place, for the servant is pouring water into the jugs in the foreground. Christ raises his hand in blessing, and Mary, seated right beside him, stares confidently at her Son.

When the water had been transformed into wine, the steward tasted it and remarked that it was unusual to reserve the best wine for the end of the feast rather than the beginning. Many theologians call this miraculous event at Cana Christ's "first miracle." But from Mary's perspective it was not. It is not common that a woman is visited by an angel, conceives by the Holy Spirit, and gives birth to a child while retaining her virginity. Changing water into wine would seem a small thing by comparison. But even in the comparison there are great mystical ramifications. The jars used for the miracle were *immaculately clean*, for they were the ceremonial water jars that Jews reserved only for ritual purification. The miracle of water turning into wine in those immaculate jars parallels the miracle of Christ's Birth from the womb of the Virgin

Mary. The Gospel writer also makes a point of telling us that there were SIX jars. According to Jewish tradition, SEVEN is the number that is complete and perfect. SIX is the number that is unfinished and imperfect. Thus the six stone water jars represent the imperfections of the old Jewish law. Jesus came to do away with the imperfections of the law and to put in their place the new wine of his Gospel of grace. And finally, just as Christ sanctified the institution of marriage by his presence at the Wedding Feast at Cana, so too does this miracle of water into wine point to the sacrament of baptism that culminates in the Eucharist. Both of these sacraments are administered by Christ's own bride, which is the Church. Juan de Flandes' portrayal of Mary in this panel painting reinforces our notion of her as a powerful intercessor exercising enormous influence with her Son. For, as the Gospel passage attests, Christ may have felt that his time had not yet come, but he responded immediately to her plea. And so she pleads our cause as well. As we say over and over again in the *Hail Mary*, may she be an advocate for us sinners especially at the hour of our death, so that we too can enjoy that eternal feast that is prepared for us in heaven.

Supplemental Essay 2016

SCENES OF
THE PASSION

Scenes of the Passion from *The Life of Our Lord Jesus Christ* (189[...]
Jacques Joseph Tissot (1836–1902),
color and monotone prints

From the autumn of 1818 until the spring of 1824, the German Romantic poet Clemens Brentano abandoned his flourishing career as a literary light in secular society in order to keep vigil at the bedside of a stigmatized nun in Westphalia. The nun Anne Catherine Emmerich had been a celebrated figure since 1812, when she received the wounds of Christ on her body. But the mysterious wounds were not in themselves the most remarkable phenomenon surrounding the Augustinian who had been displaced from her convent by the invading forces of Napoleon. It was her amazing power of clairvoyance that attracted Brentano to her side and bolstered his newly found faith in the religion of his ancestors. For she had the gift of seeing into the past, present, and future, to a degree unequaled by any other stigmatist in history. And she claimed that God had sent him to her in order to make her visions known to the world.

Sixty years later, a French artist who had been a celebrated society painter in England lost his mistress to sudden death and was plunged into a fit of despair. Jacques Joseph Tissot returned to his native country, read Brentano's account of Anne Catherine Emmerich's revelations, and experienced a spiritual conversion. He decided to dedicate the

rest of his life to illustrating the life of Christ in the Gospels, and even visited the Holy Land in order to gain inspiration. By 1897, the resulting *Life of Our Lord Jesus Christ* had been published in several volumes, first in France and then in England and America. A total of 365 illustrations had been designed by the artist, the most powerful of which were the Passion series, a scene-by-scene account of Christ's torture and death by crucifixion.

Much of what Tissot portrayed was influenced by Brentano's account of Emmerich's mystical revelations, published in 1833 under the title *The Dolorous Passion of Our Lord and Savior Jesus Christ*. As the illustrations reflect, Emmerich's visions of the Passion of Christ are highly descriptive, giving artists good source material and enabling viewers to feel an immediate presence to the sublime event. Tissot's images are inspired by the words of the visionary, down to their most gruesome details. This is especially true concerning the hammering of the first nail:

"A sweet, dear, spasmodic cry of anguish broke from the Lord's lips and his blood spurted out upon the arms of the executioners.... I counted the strokes of the hammer, but my anguish made me forget the number. The Blessed Virgin sobbed in a low voice, but Magdalen was perfectly crazed. Both arms had been torn from the sockets, the shoulders were distended, and hollow.... Jesus's breast heaved and his legs were drawn up doubled to his body.... The abdomen was entirely displaced, and it seemed as if the ribs broke away from the breastbone."

The newsreel-like depiction of Christ's Passion is depicted with a graphic intensity that makes still pictures come alive. This had long been perfected

in the popular newspaper *The Illustrated London News*, but it is also supported by the meticulous detail rendered in Emmerich's account itself. Throughout her visions, Christ and his Mother Mary are connected in spirit as she follows him through every stage of his suffering. Tissot pictures her as the Sorrowful Mother, ever weeping, with arms extended or hands clasped in prayer. The Apostle John supports her heavily swathed figure which becomes a totem of sadness quaking in grief. She is portrayed here and there throughout the illustrations as just one of the many spectators present at the Crucifixion. But Tissot pictures her separately after the horror has passed as going back to the scenes of Christ's Passion, reliving them in her own memory, the earliest observance of the Stations of the Cross.

Significantly, the symbolism of salvation history is not lost in Emmerich's visions. With the raising of the cross, so dramatically portrayed in Tissot's illustration, the visionary sees the sacrifice on Calvary paralleling the Passover sacrifice going on at the same time inside the Temple precincts in Jerusalem:

"The position of the sun at the time of Jesus's crucifixion showed it to be about a quarter past twelve, and at the moment the cross was lifted the trumpet of the Temple resounded. The Paschal Lamb had been slaughtered."

Minute by minute, hour by hour, the watch at the Passion proceeds. Angelic seraphim mark the passing of time with a clock.

During the mocking of Christ the crowd is shown surging forward, taunting Christ and those dear to him who are forced out of the way:

"Twelve Pharisees, twelve Sadducees, twelve scribes, and some of the ancients likewise rode up the mount.... They rode around the circle and drove away the Blessed Virgin, calling her a dissolute woman.... They wagged their heads contemptuously, saying Fie on you, liar! How do you destroy the Temple and build it again in three days?... The soldiers, in like manner, mocked and said, If you are the King of the Jews, help yourself now!"

In Tissot's illustrations the sky turns dark, but the activity on Calvary becomes highlighted by a mysterious luminescence. The prints look cinematic, as if they were storyboards for a movie. (Indeed many a movie-maker has referred to them throughout the history of cinema). Yet despite all their immediacy and their realism, Tissot was not afraid to shy away from inserting images of the miraculous and the marvelous. In one print called *It is Finished!* the artist surrounds the crucified Redeemer with the spirits of prophets from the Old Testament. They are suspended in space and they hold aloft the Scripture that is fulfilled here by this sacrifice. All the drama and the pathos of the Passion story spills over the page in a medley of printed word and picture. It was Tissot's most ambitious work, and one that crowned his spiritual conversion.

Passion narratives have a long tradition in Catholic culture. But none of them have had the wrenching drama and artistic staying power as this one, which was first envisioned by a stigmatic nun, written by a Romantic poet, and designed by a society painter turned Gospel illustrator.

Art Essay Holy Week 2002

LA DOLOROSA

La Dolorosa (1680–1689),
Cristóbal de Villalpando (c. 1649–1714),
oil on canvas, 83.4 x 54.9 in.

At the Cross her station keeping,
Stood the mournful Mother weeping
Close to Jesus to the last.

Thus begins the English version of the venerable Latin sequence known as the *Stabat Mater*. Mary, standing underneath the cross, witnessing and participating in her Son's Passion, fulfills the prophecy pronounced by Simeon in the Temple when he took the Baby Jesus in his arms, declared him to be the glory of Israel, but ominously predicted to the Virgin that he would also be *a sign spoken against,* adding that a sword should pierce her own soul (cf. Lk 2:35).

That sword plunging through the very heart of the Sorrowful Mother (*La Dolorosa*) is somberly depicted here in a dramatic interpretation by the 17th-century Mexican artist Cristóbal de Villalpando. Surrounded by seven archangels who are equally mournful, the Queen of Angels cannot be consoled, for the earthbound memory of her Son's torturous death haunts her with the unremitting pain of a piercing dagger. Her desolation is compared to that which was foreseen in the Lamentations of Jeremiah (2:13): *To what can I liken or compare you, O daughter Jerusalem? What example can I show you for your comfort, virgin daughter Zion? For great as the sea is your downfall; who can heal you?*

In the clouds of memory above the Blessed Mother, infant angels known as *putti* hold two relics of Christ's Passion, his cross and the veil of Veronica, on which the face of Christ was imprinted. Down below, other relics connected with his Passion are gathered around her: the ewer and pitcher with which Pilate washed his hands, the insignia "INRI" which had been posted atop the cross, a metal glove that had struck Christ's face, the dice cast in the distribution of his garments, and the pillar and scourges used in the flagellation.

A 3rd-century theologian of the early Greek Church, Origen, postulated that the sword piercing Mary's soul signified the doubt she may have experienced when Christ, after having been foreseen by Simeon as the glory of Israel, suffered a cruel and ignominious death. By the 6th century, however, this theory had been debunked by the eastern Fathers of the Church, and the Virgin gradually assumed the image of the faithful and loving Mother trusting in God as she stood beneath the cross of death. From the 6th to the 10th centuries, the Eastern Church developed considerably the theme of Mary's sorrow, and it was thereafter embraced and developed in the West. Most of the sorrows of Mary, which have variously numbered from five to fifteen, center on the Passion and death of Christ. The celebrated "Seven Sorrows of

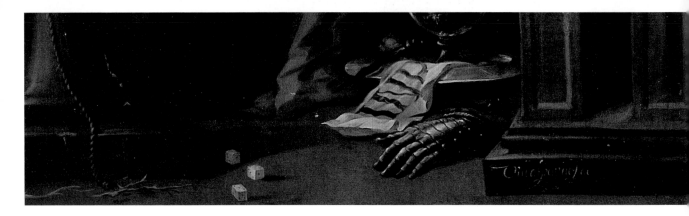

Mary" is a special devotion promoted by the Servite Order, and they include: The Presentation in the Temple, the flight into Egypt, the loss of the Christ Child in the Temple, the meeting of Jesus and Mary on the way to Golgotha, the Crucifixion, the deposition, and the burial of Jesus.

The Church calls Mary the Queen of Martyrs because her martyrdom surpassed that of all others. Although her body was not mutilated by torturers, her heart was pierced by the sword of motherly compassion for her Son. Saint Bernardine of Siena said that the sorrow of Mary was so great that if it had been equally divided among all men, they would have died of grief immediately. And an angel revealed to Saint Bridget of Sweden that if our Lord had not miraculously sustained his mother, she could not possibly have survived her martyrdom.

Here in Villalpando's painting, an archangel standing on the right holds in his hand the scepter of the Sorrowful Mother. It is the palm of martyrdom! The unity of the suffering shared between the Blessed Mother and her Son is depicted elsewhere in Passion imagery by the way the bodies of Mary and Jesus will often correspond. If Jesus is portrayed slumped over as his dead body is removed from the cross, so too the slumped-over body of the fainting Virgin is often depicted below being held up by the Apostle John. As Jesus swoons in agony and death, so Mary swoons in empathetic suffering and compassion. In witnessing the torture and death of her beloved Son, Mary's own sufferings were increased. As Richard of St. Victor explains it: "With martyrs, the intensity of their love mitigates their sufferings, but with Mary it was different; the more she loved, the more she suffered, and the greater was her martyrdom."

Tears streaming down her face, a dark veil covering her furrowed brow, the sword of sorrow struck into her nurturing breast, these are the attributes of *La Dolorosa*, and they invite us to contemplate the price at which our redemption was achieved. Meditation on the sufferings of Christ and his Blessed Mother was a special devotion of Pope Pius IX, and he felt that by contemplating such painful things the sinner would be converted and drawn to repentance. For this purpose, in 1847 he approved an alternative "Hail Mary" composed specifically to invoke the aid of the sorrowful Mother of the crucified Jesus. It reads as follows:

Hail Mary, full of sorrows,
the crucified is with thee;
thou art pitiable amongst women,
and pitiable is the fruit of thy womb, Jesus!
Holy Mary, Mother of the crucified,
implore for us, the crucifiers of thy Son,
tears of contrition,
now and at the hour of our death.
Amen.

CHRIST APPEARING TO HIS MOTHER

Christ Appearing to His Mother (1442–45), Rogier van der Weyden (c. 1399–1464), right panel of the *Miraflores Altarpiece*, oil on wood, 27.9 x 16.9 in.

The *Miraflores Altarpiece* is a celebrated triptych of the Virgin that shows three of the most affecting moments of her life: the Birth of Jesus, the Death of Jesus, and his first appearance after his Resurrection, given to her privately. It is this third scene in this Marian panoply that stirs our special interest, for we wonder where the Blessed Mother was that morning when Mary Magdalen and others discovered the empty tomb.

There is no mention in Scripture of her whereabouts, and she is not singled out as one of the specific individuals to whom Christ made an appearance. But while the Gospel says nothing, Christian tradition has long taken it for granted that Christ appeared to his Mother first. For it is logical that she who had shared most in his Passion should also share in his glory. This opinion has been held by the Doctors of the Church and by the faithful at large from the earliest times. In the 5th century, the author Sedulius maintained that in the splendor of his risen life Christ first revealed himself to his Mother. For at the Annunciation she was the means by which he entered the world; likewise she would be the first to witness his entry into glory. Bathed in that glory of the Risen One, she anticipates the Church's splendor.

According to a popular 13th-century work called *Meditations on the Life of Christ*, the Virgin was alone kneeling in her room when her resurrected Son appeared to her. That is how the artist has portrayed her. But in light of Sedulius' balanced equation of the Annunciation with the appearance of the resurrected Christ to his Mother, it is intriguing to note that the artist has arranged the composition in a way that has a deeper meaning. The two figures here are posing in the same way as the figures would pose in an Annunciation scene. In place of an angel bringing the Virgin the glad tidings that she will bear the Son of the Most High, Christ himself stands and brings his kneeling Mother the glad tidings of his Resurrection. The two events act as bookends of revelation in Mary's life, and the artistic rendering of the scene here evokes that earlier event.

Christ shows Mary his wounds, and she raises her hands in wonder, with tears of joy running down her cheeks. She is dressed in blue, signifying her unshakeable faith in God; her cloak is trimmed with the words of the *Magnificat* emblazoned in

gold: *My soul proclaims the greatness of the Lord; my spirit rejoices in God my Savior. For he has looked upon his handmaid's lowliness; behold, from now on will all ages call me blessed. The Mighty One has done great things for me....* (Lk 1:46-49). Above her in the arch, and colored likewise in celestial blue, floats an angel bearing a crown. The banderole flowing from it has an inscription alluding to a passage found in the Book of Revelation (6:2): *This woman endured and conquered all; to her was given the crown.*

Each of the three panels of the *Miraflores Altarpiece* is shaped like a church door, arranged as a portal to Paradise. Each of the doors is likewise decorated with sculptural flourishes. Painted in grisaille, the decorative archivolts on this right panel painting contain little scenes of episodes in the life of the Virgin: three holy women with the Virgin, the Assumption, Pentecost, the Announcement of Mary's death, the death of the Virgin, and Mary's coronation in heaven. On either side of the arch we see figures standing on pedestals with elaborate baldachins over their heads. On the right is Saint Paul with a sword in his hand, and on the left is Saint Mark with his attribute, the lion, resting at his feet. They are part of an overall decorative assemblage within the altarpiece that evokes the four evangelists along with Saints Peter and Paul, who all attest to the resurrection appearances of the Lord. Through

the window in the background one can see a landscape in which the Resurrection is actually taking place. Christ rises from the tomb as guards lay all around him. And in the distance beyond that, the three women begin their journey to the sepulcher bringing spices to anoint Christ's body. The Blessed Mother had no need to join them. His glorified body was already with her, hers being the first of over five hundred apparitions made by Christ to his disciples between the Resurrection and the Ascension.

The *Miraflores Altarpiece* was painted for the Carthusian monastery of that name, which contained a royal mausoleum. Thus the theme of the triptych, the cycle of life, was fitting for a chapel devoted to the dead. And it is to Mary that we pray for help at the hour of our death. That association recalls the words of Saint John Paul II, who, at a general audience on May 21, 1997, spoke the following words:

> Present at Calvary on Good Friday (see Jn 19:25) and in the Upper Room on Pentecost (see Acts 1:14), the Blessed Virgin too was probably a privileged witness of Christ's Resurrection, completing in this way her participation in all the essential moments of the Paschal Mystery. Welcoming the risen Jesus, Mary is also a sign and an anticipation of humanity, which hopes to achieve its fulfillment through the resurrection of the dead.

In the Easter season, the Christian community addresses the Mother of the Lord and invites her to rejoice: "*Regina Cæli, laetare, Alleluia!*" Thus it recalls Mary's joy at Jesus' Resurrection, prolonging in time the *rejoice* that the Angel addressed to her at the Annunciation, so that she might become a cause of *great joy* for all people.

PENTECOST

Pentecost (1934),
Maurice Denis (1870–1943),
fresco, 55.9 x 27.8 in.,
Apse of the Church of the Holy Spirit, Paris, France

I n the 12th arrondissement of Paris stands the Church of the Holy Spirit, a massive modern hulk of reinforced concrete, fashioned in a Byzantine style that evokes the Hagia Sophia of Constantinople. It is a western church bowing to the east, a tribute to the Church militant and the missionary activity that marked so great a chapter in the history of Catholic France.

The church was built between 1928 and 1935 in an archdiocesan effort to revitalize those Catholic structures that had been damaged or destroyed in Paris from previous wars. It is here in the interior of the church that the artist, Maurice Denis, painted his largest religious work. Several stories high, it is

a fresco of Pentecost, and it cascades down the apse of the church like a hierarchical staircase, connecting heaven to earth with a glimpse of purgatory in between. With red and gold hues predominating, it is a vibrant exposé showing the Paraclete inspiring the faithful to spread the Gospel and build up the kingdom of God.

In the half-dome of the apse the Dove of the Holy Spirit points downward. In Christian iconography the most appropriate way of depicting the Holy Spirit is in the form of a dove, because that is how the Spirit reveals itself in Scripture. In times past, artists have tried to portray the Spirit as an identical figure to the other persons of the Holy Trinity, or else they portrayed the Three Persons sequentially with the Father as the Ancient of Days (as described in the Book of Daniel), the mature Christ as a man in his prime (as found in the Gospels), and the Spirit as a male youth without a beard. Modern iconographers have mistaken that beardless male youth as a female (thinking it is the female allegorical figure Sophia or Wisdom), but this representation is as egregious as that of mistaking John the Apostle, another beardless male youth, as a female in scenes of the Last Supper (e.g., *The da Vinci Code*). The Council of Trent, seeing how heresy can be spawned by art, recommended that the Holy Spirit be represented as a dove, for that representation alone is faithful to Scripture.

Around the throne of God the Seraphim gather. Their color is red, the color of love. Maurice Denis has included the red-winged Seraphim around the

dove. Red is also the color of the Holy Spirit, for it is the color of the fire that danced above the heads of the disciples as they gathered in one room in the event of Pentecost. On that occasion, they heard and felt a great wind from heaven, and the artist has indicated this by the presence of two great red curtains billowing with frenetic activity. It recalls the curtain of the Temple torn in two on the occasion of Christ's crucifixion. Here, in a new covenant, the curtains make the presence of the Spirit known. That wind used to be recreated in ancient liturgy by *flabella* fanning over the holy elements of bread and wine made ready for consecration. In the East, which still reverences that tradition today, the priest ceremoniously wafts the chalice veil over the bread and wine.

In the fresco, Mary, everlasting symbol of the Church itself, stands at the pinnacle of the assembly. Her extended arms act as lightening rods to the shafts of light emanating from above. Flames of fire crown her, the eleven apostles, and Mary Magdalene. Here the missionary thrust of the Church is born, with the Spirit animating the spread of the Gospel.

On the steps below them, Saint Paul stands with his long pointed beard and right arm raised in blessing. Fathers of the Church, from both east and west, stand on the stairs beneath him. On the left side stand the Fathers of the Latin Church with their attributes: Saint Ambrose (with bees hovering around in his head), Saint Augustine (guarding a flaming heart above his open book), Saint Jerome (clothed in red cardinal's robes), and Pope Saint

Gregory the Great (wearing a papal tiara with a dove at his shoulder). On the right stand the Fathers of the Greek Church: Saints John Chrysostom, Basil the Great, Gregory Nazienzen, and Athanasius (called "the Father of Orthodoxy"). Behind the Western Fathers St. Peter's Basilica looms in the distance, while behind the Eastern Fathers the Hagia Sophia rises in glory. These represent the "two lungs of the Church," as described by Saint John Paul II.

Below the staircase is a niche with an angel bringing solace and deliverance to souls huddled in the flames of purgatory. On either side of them are bishops, priests, religious, and lay people, gathered from the four corners of the earth, sharing in that same grace felt by those individuals in the room above, who first encountered the Spirit's presence and imparted that divine spark to the world.

SAINT LUKE DRAWING A PORTRAIT OF THE VIRGIN MARY

Saint Luke Drawing a Portrait of the Virgin (c. 1435–40),
Rogier van der Weyden (c. 1399–1464),
oil and tempera on panel, 54.1 x 43.6 in.

I n a scholarly tower, high up in the sky, an artist is engaged in the making of a sketch of the Virgin Mary and the Child Jesus. But this is no ordinary artist, just as his models are not ordinary people. This is Saint Luke, known to us as one of the four Evangelists. Saint Paul, in his letter to the Colossians (4:14), also refers to Luke as his dear friend, the physician. Here, Luke is portrayed in yet another occupation made popular by the Greeks ever since the 8th century: as an intimate confidant of Mary and a portrait artist. In fact, a tradition that started in the east and spread to the west claims that Luke was the first Christian artist.

Several venerated icons of the Virgin—all of Greek origin—survive from ancient times, all claiming to be painted by the hand of Saint Luke. One was found in the catacombs with an inscription purporting that it was "one of seven painted by Luca." The popular belief that Luke was an artist was strengthened when Pope Saint Gregory the Great carried one such icon in procession through the streets of plague-stricken Rome. That icon caused a halt to the pestilence. Stories arose that Luke had used visual aids in his preaching, and that he carried with him at all times two portraits he had made. One was of the Virgin and the other one was of Christ. These images were reportedly the cause of many miracles. It was said that so wonderful were those images that many who gazed upon them were moved to admiration and devotion. Thus, through his art many conversions were made. It is not surprising that on the basis of these popular legends, Luke was for many centuries revered as the patron saint of artists, and many painters' guilds and academies of art were dedicated to him.

Rogier van der Weyden's painting, known commonly as the *Saint Luke Madonna*, was probably fashioned as an altarpiece for the painters' guild in Brussels. It expresses the dignity and esteem that he held for his profession due to the fact that the face of Saint Luke is none other than a portrait of the artist himself. He wears a scholar's cap and a red robe (the color could symbolize the account that he died a martyr's death, being crucified with Saint Andrew). He is not sketching the Madonna and Child in an art studio. Rather, he has just stepped out of his study, where he has been writing the manuscript of his Gospel. Concealed in the shadows underneath his desk is an ox, the symbol of the saint. Why? Because, explains Saint Jerome

in his commentary on Ezekiel, in Luke's Gospel the priesthood of Christ is accentuated, and the ox is the symbol of priestly sacrifice.

Saint Luke precariously genuflects before the *Madonna Lactans*, Mary nursing the Christ Child. Luke is the privileged viewer of this intimate scene of motherly love and care. Luke's Gospel is also noted for its fuller account of Mary and the Nativity of Jesus, giving rise to the tradition that the Evangelist obtained his information from the Virgin herself. A gold and red brocade panel forms a cloth of honor behind Mother and Child, and it is suspended overhead forming a baldacchino. The timbers of the room divide the round stained glass window above into three parts. This symbolizes the three known continents of the world (at that time), over which the Gospel of Luke was preached. The tripartite division of the landscape has similar symbolic value, and it is surmised that the two figures looking over the wall into the distance are Joachim and Anne, Mary's sainted parents.

Saint John Paul II saw fit to replace Saint Luke as the patron of artists with the Dominican painter Fra Angelico, whose accomplished work is verifiable. But in September of 1998 a team of scientists opened the alleged tomb of Saint Luke found in the Basilica of St. Justina in Padua and performed DNA tests upon the remains. Tradition tells us that Saint Luke was born in Antioch and died at the age of 84, around the year 150, in the Greek city of Thebes. In 338 his coffin was moved to the Byzantine capital of Constantinople, and later it was moved to Padua, Italy. Historians believe it may have been moved to Padua for safekeeping when the eastern empire was wracked with iconoclastic controversies in the 8th century, and many religious images and objects were destroyed. A record of the tomb in Padua exists as far back as 1177, and it was last opened in 1562. But interest in the saint's remains was again stirred in 1992 when the Orthodox Metropolitan of Thebes requested that part of the saint's relics be donated to the site of Luke's empty tomb in Greece. The bishop of Padua considered the request, but not until a scientific investigation of the relics had been undertaken. What scientists discovered was that the remains were indeed those of a man who had died between 70 and 85 years old, and that the body was compatible genetically with body types found in ancient Antioch. Coins and parchments found inside the tomb further supported the belief that the remains were those of Saint Luke. Thus, in the Jubilee Year of 2000, and as a gesture of goodwill, Bishop Antonio Mattiazzo of Padua sent Metropolitan Hieronymus of Thebes a rib bone of the saint, allowing at least part of the body to complete the circle to its original resting place.

THE ASSUMPTION

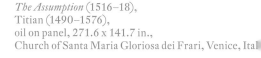

The Assumption (1516–18),
Titian (1490–1576),
oil on panel, 271.6 x 141.7 in.,
Church of Santa Maria Gloriosa dei Frari, Venice, Ital

While the dogma of the Assumption was not defined until the mid-20th century, it has been celebrated throughout the ages as part of that unique relationship between Mary and Jesus, a union that is evident in Holy Scripture, written about by the Fathers, elaborated upon by Medieval theologians, and manifest in the art and liturgy of the Church. While the Assumption is not explicitly mentioned in the Bible, Pope Pius XII used Scripture as the ultimate foundation for defining this truth. As Saint Paul states in his epistles, Christ is the New Adam. By implication, Mary is the New Eve. Just as death was brought into the world by the sin of the Old Adam, so by virtue of Christ's redemptive actions will we share in his Resurrection.

Mary was the first to do so.

Death is the penalty for sin. But, as Saint Luke states in his Gospel, the Angel Gabriel appeared to a virgin named Mary, who was apparently free from the stain of sin, for he addressed her with these words: *Hail, favored one! The Lord is with you* (Lk 1:28). In other words, it is both scripturally and reasonably apparent that Mary, being the Virgin Mother of Christ, was being prepared in grace by God to be intimately joined to her divine Son, sharing in his life. The Old Eve helped bring sin and death into the world, and shared with Adam the penalties for their offense. But, through Mary's maternity, we gain the means of our redemption. And it is fitting that Mary, free from sin like her Son, Jesus, should also share in his proximate resurrection. In the Book of Revelation (12:1-18) we gain a vision, many believe, of that cosmic resurrection awaiting the Church and personified in Mary, who is seen in the heavens as a woman clothed with the sun, the moon under her feet, and her head crowned with twelve stars.

In art, images of the Assumption go as far back as the 9th century. When Titian was commissioned in 1516 by the Franciscans of Venice to paint an Assumption of Mary as the centerpiece of the high altar in their most important church in that city, it was the first public commission of his career that he had carried out in oils. He was in his youth, and he completed it in the shortest space of time. But it was not without its difficulties. He was annoyed by the constant visits of the friars, who often complained that the artist had made the apostles too big. They were not convinced when he explained that the figures were in proportion to the vast space in which they were to be seen and that, once placed in position over the high altar, they would diminish in size from the viewer's position. It took the Ambassador of the Holy Roman Emperor to intercede and explain to the friars their erroneous thinking, and when he offered to buy the painting for his

Imperial Majesty the friars' criticism ceased. They decided to keep it for their church, declaring that they were better experts at the breviary than they were in painting. One of the art critics of the time looked at the finished work and declared, "Titian discerned and apprehended the essence of perfect painting." Today the Assumption can be seen as Titian intended it to be seen. It is the focal point of the cavernous Gothic interior of the Frari basilica. It is painted in a grand manner, with a symphony of figures stretching upward. In the lower half of the painting, an earthbound temporal zone, the crowded figures of the apostles—larger than life-size yet boldly foreshortened—gesture emphatically against a cold blue sky streaked with clouds. They display gladness and amazement at the miracle unfolding above them.

There in the upper half of the painting, in the glowing brilliance of the celestial zone, the noble figure of the Virgin is borne up in golden light. Her bodily flight heavenward delicately flutters her tunic while her cape dramatically billows with excitement. Her outstretched arms evoke the *orans* position—that liturgical pose of ancient Christians at prayer—and embrace the vision she wondrously perceives. Her face, so often rendered as young and lovely, is highlighted here with the sublime and powerful expression of rapture. All around her cherubs gather and frame her body as she is lifted on high in an explosion of clouds, wings, musical instruments, and radiant luminosity.

The source of that radiant luminosity is the figure of God the Father, who literally glides down from the celestial realm to greet the Mother of his Son.

Yet one last question remains, a question that is not addressed in this painting. If death is a consequence of sin, did the sinless Mary actually die before she was assumed into heaven? Pope Pius made no judgment on this subject, and it is a question that has puzzled theologians from the earliest times. A feast of the "Dormition" of Mary—that is, her falling asleep as in death—has been celebrated in the Eastern Church since the 6th century, and in the West soon after. While no definite consensus has been reached on this issue, most theologians have reasoned that Mary did in fact die. Although she was free from sin, she belonged to a fallen human nature and inherited from it a mortal human body. And it seems fitting that she, who conformed all things to Christ, ought to have likewise tasted death in imitation of her divine Son, whose Resurrection and Ascension she gloriously imitates in her Assumption.

Art Essay August 2003

ST. JOHN ON PATMOS GAZING AT A VISION OF THE APOCALYPSE

Saint John on Patmos Gazing at a Vision of the Apocalypse (1474–79), Hans Memling (c. 1433–1494), right panel of the *Triptych of Saint John the Baptist and Saint John the Evangelist*, oil on panel, 69.3 x 31.1 in.

sky were itself a stage. In contrast, the Eastern Church usually portrays John on Patmos as an old man sitting in a dark cave dictating his mystical visions to an assistant.

Memling's primary focus in this apocalyptic spectacle is a vision of heaven enclosed by two circular rainbows wherein the Lord sits enthroned surrounded by elders wearing white robes and gold crowns. While John records that the elders were all holding harps, the artist has given them instead a variety of musical instruments, as they provide orchestral accompaniment to the hymn they are about to sing (Rv 5:9-10):

> Worthy are you to receive the scroll
> and to break open its seals,
> for you were slain and with your blood
>   you purchased for God
> those from every tribe and tongue,
>   people and nation.
> You made them a kingdom and priests
>   for our God,
> and they will reign on earth.

The Mystic Lamb gently rests his front limbs on the lap of the Lord, ready to unseal the Book that will usher in the end times and bring forth cosmic disasters. These are already beginning to occur in the landscape below as the four horsemen ride forward, bringing with them a variety of scourges. First, there is a white horse whose crowned rider carries a bow ready to unleash an arrow. This is interpreted as Pestilence, for in the ancient world it

One thinks of John, the Beloved Disciple, as a young beardless man, for that is how he is usually painted in scenes depicting the life of Christ. But tradition holds that later in his long life he was exiled to the island of Patmos, where he recorded the mystical revelations he received there, turning the young Apostle and Evangelist into a venerable old Prophet. The Flemish artist Hans Memling portrays John as bearded yet still full of youthful vitality in this panel of a larger triptych. The saint sits on his little island and gazes upward as he records the incredible images presented to him as if the

was believed that the gods spread plague through arrows shot from heaven. The second horse is red with a rider carrying a sword. This is interpreted as War, brandishing the instrument that has become the symbol of violence and slaughter. The third horse is black with a rider carrying scales. He is interpreted as Famine, for the scales represent the buying and selling of food. And the last horse is pale color of decay. Its skeletal rider is clearly identified as Death. Followed by the jaws of hell full of screaming reprobates, this rider has been given authority with the other horsemen to decimate one quarter of the earth.

It is a time of panic and confusion. Three men, representing the various castes of society, are seen hastily crawling into caves for refuge. Fire and smoke belch forth from the ground, locusts swarm, and armies gather. It is a time of violent earthquakes and terrifying weather.

The distant heavens, too, are filled with conflict and drama. The Book of Revelation implies that the Madonna of the Apocalypse has become the Ark of the New Covenant (Rv 11:19-12:1). The Virgin, standing on a crescent moon and enveloped by the radiant light of the sun, finds herself accosted by a seven-headed dragon. She passes her newborn Child to an angel for protection and safety.

Celestial figures battle both on earth and in the sky. They wear liturgical robes and burn incense

on the altar before the Mystic Lamb. The Great Angel stands on columns of fire beneath a rainbow and a cloud filled with lightning and thunder. He holds a book in his hand and points toward the heavenly throne.

John heard the angels and the four living creatures and the elders surrounding the throne cry out in a loud voice (Rv 5:12):
Worthy is the Lamb that was slain
to receive power and riches,
    wisdom and strength,
honor and glory and blessing.

Thereupon John heard every creature in the universe respond (Rv 5:13):
To the one who sits on the throne
    and to the Lamb
be blessing and honor, glory and might,
forever and ever.

The artist has managed to juxtapose this heavenly liturgy with an apocalyptic panorama that fits neatly into an economy of space. He achieves what no artist up to that date had accomplished. Hans Memling has transposed the highlights of the entire Book of Revelation into a single landscape. But did he turn his patron saint into an alter ego? Saint John sits calmly and impassively in the foreground, as though the visions were being observed not from the outside but rather by the inner light of ecstasy.

One wonders if the artist viewed his own artistic imagination as stemming from that same source of Spirit and grace.

THE CROWNING
OF MARY

The Crowning of Mary (late 20th c.),
Mexican Anonymous, ceramic folk art.

While most of the art featured in MAGNIFICAT is "high art" produced by masters of their craft and housed in churches, palaces, and museums, there is a whole other realm of artistic representations of the Faith that the Church has appropriated and even promoted. It is considered "low art." It is often mass produced or made by amateur artisans and sold in religious article stores and pilgrimage shrines. Frequently sentimental in nature, these representations of Christ, the Virgin, and the saints have the ability to touch the heart of the owner in the same way that a teddy bear can provide security and comfort to a toddler. Folk Art can also be included in this category, and lately it has gained respectability as an expression of ethnic creativity amongst art historians. This ceramic image of Mary is a case in point.

If you were to travel eight and one-half hours by train heading west out of Mexico City, three more hours by bus, and another forty-five minutes by local transport, you would find yourself deep within the Mexican state of Michoacán, in a little village called Ocumicho. There does not appear to be anything remarkable about the village, with dusty dirt roads and compact adobe huts. Only three hundred families live there. Yet beneath its ordinary appearance, the village has become known as one of the few great producers in the country of a ceramic folk art known as "Figuras Fantasticas" (Fantastic Figures), specializing in religious art, surrealistic animals, and comic demons. For generations this has been a craft produced by the women of the village. Mothers and daughters carry on the tradition of fashioning and painting the ceramic figures inside their homes while men gather clay for them, maintain the furnaces, and help sell the work in the surrounding marketplaces. Wildly colorful, often playful and humorous, the hand-built figures of terracotta clay are fired in small wood-burning kilns, painted with water-based pigments, and varnished. It is an art form charged with optimism and devotion. Here, in a work representing the Crowning of Mary, an ancient Christian tradition is translated into a modern native idiom.

The figures are dark-skinned, like the people of the village. The Virgin's hands are folded in prayer. She is molded in the fashion of Our Lady of Guadalupe, the most renowned Marian image in Mexico. Her blue mantle is star-studded and held open by winged cherubs. Her white tunic is replete with flowers. She stands on a pink moon, whose comic

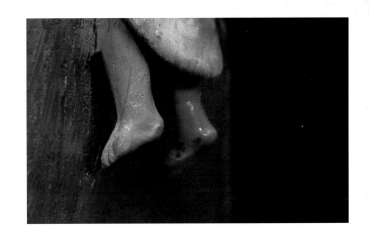

face looks up to her. An angel strains to support this heavenly retinue, while a burst of sunshine frames her entire body. This is the woman adorned with the sun and standing on the moon, as mentioned in the Book of Revelation of Saint John (12:1). Above her head, she is being crowned by a bearded and mustachioed image of God the Father, who wears the cope and miter of a bishop. On either side, identical figures wearing colorful serapes and golden caps, an evocation of God the Son and the Holy Spirit, join the Father in this celestial coronation.

The notion of Mary's Queenship is rooted in Scripture itself. At the Visitation, Elizabeth greeted Mary by calling her *the Mother of my Lord* (Lk 1:43), an Old Testament phrase for a queen-mother. Since Christ is the royal Messiah, Mary shares in a subordinate and analogous way his rule in the kingdom of grace. Her title is derived from her divine motherhood, from the excellence of her holiness, and from her cooperation with God's will in the Savior's work of Redemption. She rules with a mother's love, and by her influence over the heart of Christ she pleads with him for her spiritual children. Nations all over the world look to Mary as their heavenly Queen and interceding Mother.

For centuries, devotion to the Blessed Virgin has been a particular hallmark of Mexican piety. In this Ocumicho sculpture, the flowering cacti below recall the miracle of Tepeyac in 1531, when the native Juan Diego was instructed by Our Lady to pick flowers in the dead of winter and deliver them to the bishop. When he delivered them as instructed, the flowers fell out of his mantle (made from cactus fiber), revealing inside the garment the miraculous image of Our Lady of Guadalupe. That image of Mary as a native woman achieved in a short time what the Spanish missionaries had found difficult to accomplish: the conversion of millions of natives to the Faith.

This vibrant ceramic testimony to Mary's Queenship is not without some native humor, so typical of the Ocumicho designers. In the back of the colorful assemblage, behind the sunburst cloth of honor that acts as a backdrop for the Virgin's image, the figure of God the Father has two bare feet dangling out from underneath his ceremonial cope. The pomp and splendor of Mary's heavenly crowning remains grounded here in the familiar and earthy pictorial vocabulary of a native artisan.

THE FEAST OF
THE ROSE GARLANDS

The Feast of the Rose Garlands (1506),
Albretch Dürer (1471–1528),
oil on panel, 63.7 x 76.6 in.

At first sight one can see that this is a deeply religious painting. The rosary devotion began with garlands of roses strung together in honor of the Virgin Mary. Legend has it that Saint Dominic received the rosary chaplet directly from our Lady. Historically, it has been promulgated by the Order of Preachers. Since the later part of the 15th century in Germany, lay confraternities were especially formed to foster this kind of prayer, and the artist has used the theme to identify the popular devotion especially with his native country. In Dürer's painting the Madonna and Child are enthroned before a cloth of honor, and they each pass out a crown of roses. So too does Saint Dominic, who stands behind the throne in his black and white habit. The Feast of the Rose Garlands was also known as the Festival of the Rosary, and the passing out of rose garlands by Christ and Mary and little Italianate cherubs (called *putti*) connect the devotion with an authority that is indeed heaven sent!

Coming from the Gothic north, Dürer was beguiled by the humanistic tendencies that had infiltrated art and religion in Italy. In an effort to adopt that sense of balance and harmony that now ruled all things cultural south of the Alps, Dürer composed in the center of his painting a triangle of figures that stabilizes his composition and gives it a central weight and focus not found just a few years earlier, in his wildly fantastic and asymmetrical graphic illustrations to the Apocalypse. This central triangle comes to a point at the cross in the imperial crown held aloft over the Virgin's head.

I n the year 1505 a plague swept through southern Germany, causing Albrecht Dürer, the foremost engraver of his day, to seek refuge in Venice. While there he hoped to prove to the Italians that he was more than just a graphic artist. He wanted to paint an excellent German painting that could compete with the finest Italian Renaissance masters. The theme that he chose was *The Feast of the Rose Garlands.*

Two kneeling figures with flowing robes on either side of the throne complete the triangle. On the left kneels Pope Julius II, whose papal tiara has been placed on the ground as he lowers his bare head and receives a garland from the Christ Child. On the right is the German King Maximilian, his crown likewise doffed in favor of the garland given to him by the Virgin.

All is a picture of devotion, piety, and peace, as a Spanish saint, an Italian pope, and a German monarch meld into one serene and sublime composition where heaven and earth unite and noble figures kneel to pray.

But there is a tension in this painting, both seen and unseen. Outside the stabilizing triangle used so often in Renaissance painting, the rest of the figures seem Medieval in their crowded and cramped assembly. Except for the cardinal kneeling behind the pope, most of these figures depicted were merchants. That is understandable, seeing that the painting was commissioned by a group of German merchants living in Venice. While the artist incorporated into his painting the spectacular violets, reds, and blues favored by the Italians, both the vegetation and the landscape are German, sketched no doubt by Dürer as he journeyed from his homeland to Venice.

Where Dürer came from, artists were still largely thought of as craftsmen. But in Italy they were more and more revered as celebrity figures inspired by God. In his own day, Michelangelo would walk the streets and be hailed by the populace as *il divino*. In contrast to northern Europe, torn as it was by religious strife, peasant revolts, and a reformist horror of religious imagery, artists

like Dürer felt greater comfort and respect south of the Alps. Yet despite all of the advantages he experienced in Italy, Dürer was a German to the very core of his being. He even included in this painting a portrait of himself, leaning against a distant tree at the far right. In his hand he holds a sheet of paper that identifies him as the author of the painting. And after his name he inscribed the word *Germanus*.

For all of the Italianate flourishes exercised in this work, the underlying tenor of the painting identifies itself with German interests. Beneath that spiritualized ideal lies a political message. The Hapsburg King Maximilian had long desired to be elected Holy Roman Emperor, something neither the pope nor the King of France nor the Venetians had wanted to see happen. But it did, and the German merchants wanted to convey in this painting the idea that Christendom would be safe under Hapsburg rule. Despite the political spin underlying the spiritual repose of the painting, it did not stop the Doge and the Patriarch of Venice from visiting Dürer and praising his work. Such men as these recognized that, while rulers come and go, great works of art survive the test of time.

THE FIFTEEN MYSTERIES AND THE VIRGIN OF THE ROSARY

The Fifteen Mysteries and the Virgin of the Rosary (1515–20), attributed to the Netherlandish painter Goswijn van der Weyden (1455–1543), oil on wood, 9.9 x 21 in.

Out of the garden and into the hands of millions of devout Christians, the rosary has become one of the leading meditational devices for prayer in the history of the Church. The word "rosary" originally referred to a garden where roses grow. But today the word refers to the chaplet or string of beads that progressively chart the mysteries of redemption. These mysteries are vividly illustrated in this early Netherlandish painting which acted as a visual aid to the chaplet prayers.

In the lower register of the painting stands the Blessed Virgin Mary with the Christ Child. They are framed by a string of roses and a baldacchino of honor. The area is also demarcated by a wall. This is an enclosed garden, a *hortus conclusus*, something that is replete with scriptural and theological symbolism. In the Song of Solomon (4:12ff) there is a vivid account of the Beloved described as *an enclosed garden, a fountain sealed*. Christians interpreted this as an image of the Blessed Virgin Mary, the Mother of God, the New Eve who would lead her children back into the Garden of Paradise that

had been lost by the first Eve, the mother of all nations. Furthermore, the enclosed garden became a symbol for Mary's womb and a sign of her perpetual virginity. In that garden, the rose stood out as the most beautiful of flowers, a plant that is continually mentioned in Scripture, associated with Mary, and seen as the only flower with sufficient beauty to express the mystery of the Incarnation. For Dante it symbolized the miracle of divine Love brought down to earth, and in the *Paradiso* of his *Divine Comedy*, heaven itself is shaped like a rose.

Let us crown ourselves with rosebuds, says the Book of Wisdom (2:8). To the Christian, garlands became a sign of heavenly joy, a return to the happiness of Paradise. When paintings like this began to appear with the Virgin and Child reposing in a garden surrounded by roses, so too strings of beads were progressively being used by the faithful to pray to Mary for her intercessory powers while meditating upon significant events in salvation history.

The red and white roses in the painting represent prayers. The red roses designate the *Paternosters* (the Our Father) and the white roses represent ten successive recitations of the *Ave Maria* (the Hail Mary). With each decade of the rosary, one mystery is meditated upon. The complete rosary canvases fifteen events drawn from Scripture and sacred tradition.[1] These include the five Joyful Mysteries (the Annunciation, the Visitation, the Nativity, the Presentation of Christ in the

Temple, and the Finding of the Child Jesus in the Temple), seen on the top register of the painting. On the middle register, the five Sorrowful Mysteries are portrayed (the Agony in the Garden, the Scourging of Christ, the Crowning with Thorns, the Carrying of the Cross, and the Crucifixion). The last triad portrays the Glorious Mysteries (the Resurrection, the Ascension, Pentecost, the Dormition and Assumption of the Virgin, and the Coronation of Mary). Down below, a tonsured figure in habit kneels before the Madonna and Child. He is accompanied by a dog with a flaming torch in its mouth. This is Saint Dominic, whose Order has propagated devotion to the rosary throughout the centuries. The dog is a pun on his name and a symbol of his Order (the *Domini canes*, hounds of the Lord). The flaming torch represents the light of truth. Behind Dominic kneels a pope, an emperor, and a king. These represent the Christian Estates, men of power supplicating the Virgin of the Rosary on behalf of those entrusted to their care.

On the other side of the painting the Christ Child leans over to bless a man kneeling while assassins are about ready to kill him. This is a reference to a legend wherein a knightly gentleman escaped death by the intervention of the Virgin of the Rosary. Out of the kneeling man's mouth, prayers usher forth in the shape of roses. *Let my prayer arise before you like incense,* says the Psalmist (141:2a). So, too, this man's prayers take the form of fragrant roses. The connection between the garden and the rosary was so great that people often fashioned the beads of their chaplets from a compound made from fragrant flowers, herbs, and spices. Others would attach perfumed pomanders to their rosaries. In that way the senses were invited to take an active part in the devotional exercise. In meditating, one could imagine smelling the very flowers of Paradise!

In the Garden of the Rosary, scent itself becomes a metaphor for the sweetness of prayer.

[1] Editor's note: The writing of this essay, like the painting of this masterpiece, preceded Saint John Paul II's 2002 announcement of the Luminous Mysteries.

Art Essay October 2000

THE HEAVENLY ROSARY

The Heavenly Rosary (c. 1510),
Hans von Kulmbach (1480–1528),
central panel of the *Triptych of the Rosary*,
oil on panel, 46.1 x 33.2 in.

The cross of Christ, that profound symbol of redemption, casts its shadow over all of Holy Week. Here it is also the central focus of a complex painting, a standard which dissects a four-tiered assemblage of figures surrounded by a circle of roses. But these are no mere roses. Five decades of silver roses punctuated by five cruciform golden roses turn this floral frame into a fragrant rosary of fifty *Ave Marias* and five *Paternosters*. The five cruciform roses allude to the five wounds of Christ. In fact, it is the body of Christ, broken and bleeding, which is the singular object of devotion in this detailed work of art. So, too, the five Sorrowful Mysteries act as a fulcrum to the larger fifteen-decade rosary, which includes Joyful and Glorious Mysteries. The artist would seem to be saying that by meditating upon these sacred mysteries, the diligent soul can aspire to a vision of heaven itself. For as we look closer, the array of figures inside this heavenly rosary are saints and angels of Paradise, radiating in groups around the *throne of grace*, constituted by the vertical axis of Father, Son, and Holy Spirit.

On the highest tier to the right of God the Father is the Madonna holding her infant Son. Angels attend to the figures in this lofty sector. Beneath the Madonna are patriarchs and prophets of the Old Testament: Melchizedek who was the priest–king of Salem, King David with his harp, the horned Moses carrying the tablets of the Law, and John the Baptist who prepared the way for the Lamb of God. The rest of the grouped figures follow roughly the categories of saints as found in the Roman Missal and celebrated in the liturgy. On the right are Apostles and Evangelists: Peter with his keys and Paul with his sword. Between them is Mark, who journeyed with both of them and wrote his own Gospel. At the end is the evangelist Luke, accompanied by an ox.

The "attribute" of a saint is the sign or insignia that visually identifies the figure we are looking at. In times of illiteracy, these visual indicators enabled the faithful to recognize the saint and recall his or her legend. This is particularly helpful in von Kulmbach's painting when we look at the sector of the martyrs. There is Lawrence, holding the gridiron upon which he was roasted. Next to him stands the armored soldier–martyr George. The bishop–martyr Erasmus holds his entrails on a winch. The deacon Stephen is identified by the stones that

pummeled him to death, and the little infant holding a red cross is one of the Holy Innocents. Behind the martyrs are palm branches, an award of victory for their ultimate sacrifice.

Across from the martyrs stand Doctors and confessors of the Church: Gregory the Great with his papal tiara, Jerome wearing cardinal's attire, the bishop Nicholas carrying three clumps of gold, and an aged, bearded king (without an attribute he could be Charlemagne or some other revered monarch). At the foot of the cross are the virgins: Clare with her monstrance, an unidentified maiden, Barbara holding a chalice, and Catherine of Alexandria with her broken wheel and sword. Holy women who are not virgins complete the heavenly circle: Anne with Mary and the Baby Jesus, Mary Magdalene with her spice jar, and the Empress Helen bearing the true cross.

In this panoply of the blessed, one returns to the figure of the Blessed Virgin Mary, with whom the Rosary is so intimately associated. Titles of honor found in her litany are exquisitely visualized in this composition, for Mary is invoked as Queen of Angels, Queen of Patriarchs, Queen of Prophets, Queen of Apostles, Queen of Martyrs, Queen of Confessors, Queen of Virgins, and Queen of All Saints. All these categories are represented here, comprising a heavenly host encircled by the ensign of the Mother of God.

These figures also represent diverse lives dedicated to the same ultimate end—the Beatific Vision and everlasting happiness. Within the circle of

eternity they reign triumphant. But outside the circle there are scenes of judgment and suffering. At the lower left St. Michael, holding a scale, weighs a pleading soul pitted against devilish pleasures. On the lower right numerous souls writhe in purgatory while an angel lifts a purified spirit (born anew to a new life and thus represented as a baby) up toward the blissful circle of heaven.

Christ told his followers that they must take up their own crosses in imitation of him. This is a particularly potent meditation for Passiontide. But one must remember that the making of a Christian hero entails not just courage and wisdom and sacrifice but also contemplation and prayer. The wheel of the rosary is a means of achieving that, as it fixes our attention on the sublime mysteries of salvation.

Art Essay Holy Week 2000

THE VISION OF SAINT BERNARD

The Vision of Saint Bernard (1504), Fra Bartolomeo (1472–1517), oil on panel, 83.8 x 86.6 in.

Before Fra Bartolomeo (nicknamed Baccio) joined the Dominican Order, he had been an ardent disciple of the firebrand preacher Savonarola. He was spellbound by the apocalyptic warnings proclaimed from the pulpit at San Marco by the controversial friar, who condemned the citizens of Florence for their decadent ways and artists in particular for adopting pagan themes while their religious works lacked humility and reverence. Baccio participated in "The Bonfire of the Vanities," whereupon artists who had a change of heart submitted their secular and irreverent works to the flames. He even barricaded himself inside the Dominican priory of San Marco with 500 other supporters when it was stormed by a mob opposed to the theocrat's mystical rule of the republic. Baccio promised God that he would become a friar himself if his life were spared. He survived only to see his hero tried,

hanged, and burned at the stake in 1498. He had once painted a portrait of Savonarola as a prophet. Now, chastened by his vow, Baccio donned the cowl of a Dominican and withdrew from making art for a number of years.

The Vision of Saint Bernard marks Fra Bartolomeo's return to art in 1504. The friar was commissioned to paint it as an altarpiece for a nobleman's private chapel. In this work he brings to the subject matter an austerity of style that is reflective not only of Savonarola's views on sacred art, but those of Saint Bernard as well.

Saint Bernard of Clairvaux (1090–1153) was the dynamo behind the Cistercian reform, a movement within the Benedictine family to return to the rigors of its primitive rule. A theologian, judge, diplomat, preacher, poet, mystic, and advocate of Marian devotion, Bernard left his imprint on art history by disagreeing with the sumptuousness advocated by Abbot Suger, whose monastery chapel of Saint Denis on the outskirts of Paris exemplified the new dazzling effects of Gothic art and architecture. Suger believed that only the finest embellishments are worthy of sacred space, and he decorated his sanctuary with golden vessels, stained glass, carved capitals, tapestries, and lustrous vestments. Suger felt that more is better! But Bernard found such finery a distraction to the contemplative soul, stunting the imagination and making it passive before the dazzling effects of art. For Bernard, then, less is better for the soul, and he

advocated a kind of artistic minimalism that could prompt but not derail a prayerful monk toward contemplation of things beyond the material world. In Cistercian monasteries clear glass was preferred over stained glass windows, silver was substituted for gold vessels, walls and vestments were unadorned. One could go so far as to say that Bernard presaged the aesthetics of Protestantism, the Enlightenment, and Modernism as early as the 12th century. But one thing is clear: in their advocacy for a sobriety and noble simplicity in art, qualities that would enkindle devotion and reverence in the viewer, Savonarola and Bernard were kindred spirits. Fra Bartolomeo's painting reflects this.

When he was the prior of San Marco, Savonarola created visual images in his homilies to great effect, and he encouraged those Dominicans not gifted in oral preaching to pursue the study of the plastic arts in order that they might preach visually in ways that could distill complex theological ideas into beautiful and simple images. It was his idea that God and man ought to communicate through art, but it was art's role to be pure and chaste in this sacred venture, and be free of all useless artifice and ornamentation.

Bartolomeo's rendition of Saint Bernard's vision of the Virgin Mary is far less fussy than an earlier rendition of the subject painted by Filippino Lippi in 1485. The Dominican has anchored the right side of his painting with three saintly figures standing before a landscape: Benedict, whose

ideals Bernard sought to rekindle; John the Apostle, whose custody of the Blessed Virgin Mary was mandated from the cross (a miniature scene depicting the Crucifixion is included here as a painterly footnote); and the kneeling Bernard, who preferred the spiritual inspiration found in nature to that found in the dusty tomes of monastic libraries. The stigmatization of Saint Francis of Assisi and his meeting with Saint Dominic are tiny visual quotations lost in the decorative hills behind these three figures. But the overwhelming majesty of the Madonna and Child borne aloft by angels on the transcendental left-hand side of the painting accentuates the fact that Bernard's vision was the product of an intense and direct contemplation of the Mother of God, using no artifice as its springboard. In fact, the sensuality that Bernard disclaimed in the material decoration of Suger's church is ironically surpassed by the sensuality that arises in some of his own mystical visions.

For instance, a more common iconographic motif of Bernard's apparition of the Virgin is based on an ecstatic encounter that happened to him in Speyer Cathedral in 1146. In that vision Bernard beseeched Mary to be his mother too, and it is recorded that the Virgin took her breast and expressed her milk onto his lips, fortifying the eloquence of his preaching. This imagery is known as the *Lactation of Saint Bernard*, and it became more popular than the staid vision depicted here by Baccio. If such flamboyant phantasms are a by-product of monastic austerity, it was not Fra Bartolomeo's aim to imitate it. His noble restraint in this painting can be attributed squarely to Savonarola's proprietary influence on his work. Later, however, Dominicans of the more extravagant Baroque era borrowed that popular lactation motif from the Cistercians and applied it visually to their equally eloquent founder, Saint Dominic, proving that while artistic styles come and go and reforming influences wax and wane, a good story can be shared, and it lasts forever.

MATER MISERICORDIÆ SHELTERING THE CARTHUSIANS

Mater Misericordiæ Sheltering the Carthusians (c. 1655),
Francisco de Zurbarán (1598–1664),
oil on canvas, 105.1 x 126 in.

Zurbarán's painting of the *Mater misericordiæ* takes an archetypal image of the Virgin Mary and particularizes it for the Carthusians, reputedly the most austere Order within the Catholic Church. Founded by Saint Bruno in 1084, the Order's first establishment was on a barren and rocky hollow near the summit of a mountain not far from Grenoble called La Grande Chartreuse, hence the origin of their name. Hermetic by nature, the Carthusians are noted for their rigorous seclusion, hair shirts, sparse meatless diet, disciplined habits of labor and prayer, and perpetual silence. Renowned also for their fine libraries (Saint Bruno felt that books should feed the soul) and their skill in gardening, the Carthusians were some of Europe's first and greatest horticulturalists, and it is said that wherever they settled they made the barren wastes blossom like a rose (a medicinal formula of herbs and spices drawn from their cloister survives today in the popular liqueur known as Chartreuse). While relatively small in number, by the 17th century the Carthusians had numerous foundations, some of which were richly decorated in the manner of the Counter-Reformation Church. It was to one of these foundations in Spain, the monastery of Santa Maria de las Cuevas near Seville, that Zurbarán was called. For them he created three canvases, each extolling one of the characteristics of their life: their veneration of Mary, their practice of abstinence from meat, and their vow of silence. The artist studied the monks for several months, and a bond of trust and understanding was established.

No one could paint monks like Francisco de Zurbarán. His ability to take the religious habit and translate its intricate folds and broad planes into totemic volumes radiating the Baroque spirituality of imperial Spain was unparalleled. No wonder the Dominicans, Franciscans, Mercedarians, Trinitarians, Hieronymites, Carmelites, and Carthusians commissioned him to glorify their saints. Even the French Romantics and anticlericals of the 19th century and the surrealists of the 20th came to adore his simplicity, his ravishing color, and his oftentimes bizarre juxtapositions as proto-modernist in style.

In painting the *Mater Misericordiæ Shelter-ing the Carthusians*, Zurbarán chose an image of our Lady that dates to the middle of the 13th century. Cistercian in origin and quickly adopted by the Dominicans and others, it shows the Blessed Mother as Queen of Heaven, extending her cloak of protection over her chosen ones on earth. What is particularly interesting in this canvas is the allusion to the rosary, a devotion that the Carthusians claimed was theirs prior to its popularization by the Dominican preacher and teacher Alanus de Rupe in 1460. It was then that Blessed Alanus had claimed to have received visions of Saint Dominic receiving the rosary from the very hand of the Virgin herself. But the Carthusians pointed to their own monk, Dominique Hélion, established at their monastery in Trier in 1409, whom they believed first proposed a system of meditations on the life of Christ coupled with the recitation of the *Ave Maria*. Another Carthusian of the same monastery, Jean de Rhodes, further developed this manner of praying. In Zurbarán's painting the monks kneel in a foreground strewn with jasmine and roses, the latter being the flower associated with the rosary. The ascetic faces of the monks are portraits of the Carthusians living at Las Cuevas when Zurbarán visited the monastery. Their serene images are realistically rendered even to the shadowing of beards on the monks, whose rule allows them to shave only six times a year. Our Lady's hands rest directly on the heads of two Carthusians. The prior and vicar of Las Cuevas were used as models, but they are presumed to represent Dominique Hélion and Jean de Rhodes receiving a special blessing from the Virgin for having formulated their rosary from the depths of their contemplation.

Mary's melancholy gaze toward the viewer strikes a chord with the Carthusian lifestyle itself. In their own particular rite they are instructed to chant the divine office as if in lamentation. The haunting beauty of that chant was captured in the documentary film *Into Great Silence* (2005), made by a film director who, like Zurbarán, gained admittance to the monks' inner sanctum in order to study and capture a dazzling picture of the fabled recluses. In Zurbarán's painting, Mary's blue cloak is held open by cherubs. The darkened interior of

her garment, forming a protective womb or a cave of refuge, contrasts sharply with the brilliant white rendering of the monks' clothing. It is Zurbarán's delineation of those white habits that prompted another painter to declare this skill a "thing of wonder, for although they are all white, they are differentiated by their individual values. They are done with such admirable realism in the folds, color, and form that they counterfeit reality itself."

Perhaps the artist did not counterfeit reality so much as heighten it in the manner of one whose senses are held in check in order to spiritually penetrate the very nature of that reality. Here Zurbarán has captured the serene quiet of Carthusian life, its hieratic structure, its emphasis on meditation and devotion, the beauty of its solitude, the utility of its abnegation. Within the shadow of this heavenly shelter the soul prepares itself for divine seduction. Appropriately, the motto of the Order reflects the sublime idea behind its rarefied vocation: *Stat crux dum volvitur orbis*, Latin for "As the world turns, the cross stands still."

THE MADONNA OF MOUNT CARMEL

The Madonna of Mount Carmel (1721–27), Giambattista Tiepolo (1696–1770), oil on canvas, 82.7 x 255.9 in.

The origins of the Carmelite Order and its devotion to the Virgin Mary stretch back into the mists of time, when legend and symbol fortified ideals. From the pages of Scripture, the image of a holy mountain and an Old Testament prophet prefigure Christ's salvific entry into the world. In the First Book of Kings (18:42-46), there is a story of a great drought that crippled the land. Elijah climbed to the summit of Mount Carmel. He prayed and put his head between his knees. In time a small cloud rose from the sea and grew to cover the sky, and showered the earth with rain. Christians later interpreted this episode as symbolic of the Virgin Mary who, by giving the Savior to the world, was the bearer of the fount of redeeming grace. "Let the clouds rain down the Just One," reads one of the chants for the season of Advent.

Likewise, Isaiah 61:10 reads, *I rejoice heartily in the Lord,/ in my God is the joy of my soul;/ For he has clothed me with a robe of salvation,/ and wrapped me in a mantle of justice.* The Marian symbolism found in these words extends to all of God's children, for the Blessed Virgin wants to disseminate the grace and merits of her Son by clothing them with that mantle of justice. Herein lies the significance of the scapular, an expressive symbol of Mary's maternal concern for her children. The 13th-century English Carmelite Saint Simon Stock had a vision of the Virgin Mary while he was praying for his Order. In that vision, she presented him with a brown scapular and told him, "This is your privilege: whoever dies in it will be saved."

The Carmelites find their spiritual roots on Mount Carmel, where there was a long tradition of hermits living an austere life of prayer, fasting, and abstinence. The primitive Carmelites saw themselves as the heirs to the mystical tradition of the prophets of old. The earliest Carmelites wore white mantles with red stripes, symbolic of the miraculous cloak that Elijah wore and cast down–singed by the flames–to his disciple Elisha in the whirlwind of the fiery chariot (2 Kgs 2:11-13). Crusaders found the hermits living on Mount Carmel, and Alberto di Vercelli, Patriarch of Jerusalem, wrote their rule. When Muslim incursions into Palestine made it unsafe to remain on Mount Carmel, the hermits fled westward and, in time, adopted the lifestyle of

mendicant friars in Europe. Saint Teresa of Ávila, a Doctor of the Church and one of its greatest mystics, renewed the Carmelite Order's austerity by her reforms in the 16th century.

Tiepolo summarizes the panorama of Carmelite history in this early work. It was commissioned by a Carmelite confraternity in Venice that met to pray for the souls of the dead in the church of Saint Aponal. Confraternities often favored wide rectangular canvases like this, for it helped to focus their prayerful supplications. On the far left of the canvas an ecstatic soul leaps up and grabs the arm of a liberating angel while other souls languish in the murky confines of purgatory. Further to the right a procession of hooded figures, no doubt representatives of the confraternity itself, trail an attendant angel holding the crosier of Saint Alberto. The bearded old patriarch bends down in his splendid cope to kiss the abbreviated Carmelite scapular offered him by the Christ Child standing upon the altar. Saint Teresa of Ávila kneels before this vision of the Madonna and Child as they dispense Carmelite scapulars, the Virgin Mary handing hers to Saint Simon Stock as part of his habit. The white mantles worn by Saints Teresa and Simon no longer bear the red streaks worn by earlier Carmelites to denote the effects of the fiery chariot. But the prophet Elijah sits hooded on the far right of the canvas, hunched over in prayer and shrouded in a rain cloud driven by cherubs. Here are figures from the Old Testament and the New, with the Church triumphant and militant aiding by their prayers the Church suffering in purgatory. Filled with

darkness and light, the painting promotes the efficacy of prayer for the dead and protecting oneself on earth with a garment of grace.

While the cult of Our Lady of Mount Carmel had a long tradition, it witnessed an upsurge of devotion in the early 18th century, when Tiepolo began this painting. Pope Benedict XIII established the universal feast just a few years later in 1726, evoking the power of the Virgin Mary to intercede with her Son for the release of souls in purgatory. When the church of Saint Aponal was closed in 1810, Tiepolo's canvas was rolled up, crushed, and cut in two. Not until 1950 was it restored to its present state, evoking an idea that is ever beautiful and timeless.

THE MADONNA STANDING ON CLOUDS WITH SAINTS SIXTUS AND BARBARA

The Madonna Standing on Clouds with Saint Sixtus and Barbara (aka the *Sistine Madonna*) (1512–13), Raphael (1483–1520), oil on canvas, 106.3 x 79.1 in.

This painting is considered one of the most important works of Western civilization. The only painting by Raphael in Germany when it was purchased, it inspired Thomas Mann, Johann Wolfgang von Goethe, Richard Wagner, and even Friedrich Nietzsche to sing its praises. Augustus III, the absent king of Poland and elector of Saxony, is said to have moved his throne so that this painting, which he had purchased in 1734 and brought to Dresden from Italy, could have the highest honor in his state room. The artist Alfred Rethel, before he went insane, declared, "I would not swap for a kingdom the delight I have had from standing before this picture."

This was the last painting that the artist Raphael executed completely by his own hand, and it was his crowning achievement. He died six years later, at the age of thirty-seven. To honor his late uncle, Pope Sixtus IV, Pope Julius II commissioned this image in 1512 to be hung in the Benedictine basilica of San Sisto in Piacenza, a foundation that had long been patronized by the pope's family. The martyr Pope Saint Sixtus II (whose name is memorialized in the Canon of the Mass and gives this painting its informal title, the *Sistine Madonna*) was the foundation's patron saint, and the basilica proudly guarded the relics of another early Christian martyr, the virgin Saint Barbara—hence the two heavenly figures that accompany the Madonna and Child in the composition, who were deliberately included to reflect the basilica's pride of place.

An intricate geometry grounds the painting. Circles within a circle are created by the Infant's round face resting against that of his Mother. The curvature of her nurturing breast is highlighted through the thin tunic. The Virgin Mary holds her divine Son in such a way that their bodies are intertwined, his limbs curved round her supporting hands. Her veil billows away from her face as if it were a sail, creating a larger circle that frames both Mother and Child. The faint blue heads of cherubs, which create an aureole on either side of the Virgin, parallel the circular contours of the cumulous clouds beneath her feet. Likewise, the parted green velvet curtains that frame the composition create a pyramidal shape, which is repeated in the geometry of the Madonna standing between two kneeling attendants.

The artist has composed the painting in such a way that it appears to be a peek into paradise. The stage-like setting with parted curtains supports this effect. While the disturbing and haunting stares of both Virgin and Child hold the center of the painting with a gripping command, the periphery of the work becomes more relaxed, whimsical, and even humorous. Recent scholarship has discovered that inside the basilica the painting was designed to hang opposite a scene of the crucifixion. Thus the look of fear that envelops the infant Jesus reveals a natural human response to the sight of pain and death. The German philosopher Arthur Schopenhauer saw in the boy Jesus a face that was "terror-stricken," while the dramatist Friedrich Hebbel described the Christ Child as "wild, with teeth clenched, eyes blazing." The Virgin's cheek brushes against her Child's forehead in a protective and consoling gesture, yet her eyes betray a hint of that sadness that characterizes the *Mater dolorosa*, sharing in the suffering of her Son's destiny.

The figure of Pope Saint Sixtus points to the cross outside this canvas in support of that destiny. His papal tiara placed at his feet, he glances up toward the Child and rests his left hand on his breast, as if to include himself as one of the many martyrs who embraced death for the sake of the kingdom. The weighty and formal stiffness of his gold-embroidered cope contrasts sharply with the unkempt bushiness of his beard and corona. Some see a hint of Pope Julius himself in that saint's rugged

profile. His eyes are enraptured by the vision of the Madonna and Child, while his extended arm and index figure act as a visual bridge between the outside viewer and the celestial figures presented within the picture plane.

Opposite the pontiff, Saint Barbara kneels with her head bowed in serene dignity. Her exquisitely coiffed hair, a mixture of intricate curls tied by a silk ribbon, provides a sharp contrast to the wild shabbiness of Pope Sixtus. The visual shorthand that enabled medieval viewers to recognize a saint by an object drawn from her legend has been marginalized here in this masterpiece of the High Renaissance. Raphael has tucked Barbara's hagiographic attribute—that tower in which she was imprisoned by her pagan father (giving rise to the fairy tale of Rapunzel)—behind a sweep of curtain, giving the viewer just a hint of her identity.

Instead, the artist has diverted our attention to the richly adorned contours of her human form. While the gesture of Sixtus draws us into the picture and connects us upward to the Virgin and Child, the downward glance of Barbara brings our attention full circle to the object of her gaze below: the two curious angels propping themselves up on the lower border of the painting.

Legend has it that the mischievous *putti*, with their tousled hair, were inspired by two children Raphael observed staring into a baker's shop window. Since 1800 these cherubs have been singled out and copied, generating a life of their own as rock stars of commercialism. Yet they have an important part to play in the balance of the painting. These casual observers, with their air of nonchalance, diffuse the dread found at the center of the painting. Like the bowed curtain rod above, they present just enough comic relief to offset the pathos of the Mother and Child. They help make this painting a masterpiece—a union of figures tied together by the most sublime harmony of placement, color, gesture, and sentiment.

Art Essay August 2015

ALLEGORY OF THE BATTLE OF LEPANTO

Allegory of the Battle of Lepanto (c. 1572),
Paolo Veronese (1528–1588),
oil on canvas, 66.5 x 53.9 in.

The scene is a naval battle of apocalyptic proportions. Ships from the Muslim east and the Christian west clash in a flurry of timber, metal, sword, and arrow. Veronese commemorates in this painting that miraculous victory of October 7, 1571, when a Christian military force called the Holy League assembled at the urging of Pope Pius V to stem the tide of the larger Islamic forces preparing to invade Italy.

With the rise of Islam in the 7th century, Christianity had seen its territories in the eastern Mediterranean and north Africa swiftly diminish. From the sands of Arabia the followers of Mohammed conquered as far west as Spain and the borders of France. The Holy Land and its shrines fell under Muslim rule, the Crusades having had no lasting effect at winning them back. To the north the Byzantine Empire, long weakened by the Arian heresy,

finally collapsed before the scimitar in 1453. In August of 1571, as a prelude to Lepanto, the island of Cyprus tried to stem Ottoman advancement into the Mediterranean by withstanding a siege that had lasted nearly a year. When it finally fell, the Christian governor from Venice was flayed alive in the public square, his skin stuffed with straw and sent to the sultan as a trophy.

With all of Christian Europe hanging in the balance and now vulnerable to attack, Pope Pius V asked the faithful to pray the rosary and invoke the help of the Blessed Virgin Mary. He called upon Christian princes to unite and band together in order to fight the invader. Spain, Venice, several Italian city-states, and the Knights of Malta formed the Holy League under the leadership of Don Juan of Austria, an illegitimate son of King Charles V of Spain and half-brother to its reigning monarch, Philip II.

In the Veronese painting, above the clash of ships, and resting on heavenly clouds, a divine council of war takes place. Earnestly beseeching the Blessed Virgin Mary to intervene and grant victory to the outnumbered Christian force is the white-robed allegorical figure of Venice. Her face is hidden as she falls on her knees in supplication. Around her are heavenly allies, representing the military constituents that are battling below. On the far left stands Saint Peter with the Keys of the Kingdom. He represents the papacy and the Papal States. Next to him, wearing a pilgrim's cloak and

holding a traveling staff and hat, is Saint Roch, or Rocco, particularly honored in Venice. Directly beneath the Virgin kneels a crowned female figure holding a sword. This is Saint Justina, an early Christian virgin martyr on whose feast day the battle of Lepanto took place. Finally, on the far right of the grouping stands Saint Mark with his attribute, the lion. As patron saint of Venice, he represents those Venetian soldiers who fought most fiercely in the naval battle, remembering with bitterness and horror the slow and torturous death suffered by their countrymen on Cyprus just two months before.

An angelic choir provides a backdrop to the assembly of saints. One angel hurls down a fiery arrow toward the invaders. That a Christian appeal was made to heaven before the battle is not unusual. Saints have long been invoked in war, and Christian symbols had been carried into battle over the centuries, from Constantine to Joan of Arc. One of the admirals in the Holy League, Andrea Doria, had a replica of the miraculous image of Our Lady of Guadalupe mounted aboard his ship before the naval engagement.

As the battle ensued, Pope Pius was holding a meeting in Rome. Rising from his table, he beheld a vision. It was a picture of triumph. He turned to his council and told them that their prayers had been answered. Victory was won!

The battle took five hours, with the two forces clashing in a gulf off western Greece. Thirty thousand Turks perished in the conflict, compared to a third as many Christians. More than ten thousand Christian galley slaves held in the Ottoman navy were set free. It was the last major naval

battle fought solely among rowing vessels, and it was deemed the most important sea battle won for the west since Octavian defeated Antony and Cleopatra in the Battle of Actium in 31 B.C. Lepanto turned the tide, destroying Muslim naval superiority in the Mediterranean Sea. Europe was secure, at least for the time being.

In thanksgiving, the saintly pope dedicated October 7 to Our Lady of Victory and added the supplication "Help of Christians" to the Litany of Loreto. This feast was later rededicated to Our Lady of the Rosary, commemorating that powerful instrument of prayer with which no sword can compete.

ICON OF OUR LADY OF CAMBRAI

I n his book *Picasso's Mask*, the French minister of culture, André Malraux, recounted a story he had told to the famous Spanish artist concerning Bernadette Soubirous, the seer of Lourdes. The Virgin Mary had appeared to her eighteen times, and the site of the apparitions, the grim grotto of Massabielle, across from the River Gave, had been transformed into a place of wonder and hope with a miraculous spring. Afterward, the peasant girl entered the Convent of the Sisters of Charity at Nevers. While in the cloister, faithful from all over the world would send the saint pictures and statues of the Virgin, but she chucked them into a closet where she did not have to look at them. Dumbfounded, the Mother Superior asked Bernadette why she would do such a thing. Bernadette replied that none of the images looked like the Blessed Virgin Mary, and she could not abide to meditate on images that were not true.

This motivated the Mother Superior to write the bishop, who came to the convent with large picture books filled with all the well-known images of the Virgin. He showed the simple nun, who had never seen great art, images of Mary as painted by such masters as Raphael and Murillo. But Bernadette shook her head no to all of them. Then, as they were flipping through the pages at random, they came upon an image of an icon venerated in the town of Cambrai. Falling on her knees, Bernadette exclaimed to the bishop that the face she saw in that icon looked just like the face she had seen in the grotto so many times before. Malraux and Picasso later conjectured on how a simple, uneducated girl with no sophistication could possibly have seen the face of a real person in a painting that lacked depth, movement, and realistic illusion. Malraux surmised, and Picasso agreed, that there was some numinous element in primitive art that knocked on the very door of the sacred. In essence, Bernadette, who had never before seen an icon, once again came face to face with the divine.

The icon can be traced back to 1440, when it was brought from Rome to Cambrai. Saint Luke himself was reputed to have painted it, and so it was accordingly venerated and copied. Yet its Italo-Byzantine style dates it to the first part of the 14th century, placing it far from the 1st century and the biblical era. What is most probable is that the icon itself is a copy of an earlier painting now lost in the mists of time. It exudes a spiritual power of its own, nevertheless, one that attracted Bernadette's eye and made her drop to her knees.

In the Byzantine tradition, the icon is a type known as the Virgin "Eleousa," which highlights the affection and intimacy between Mother and Child. Mary holds the Christ Child close to her

face. They press against each other, cheek to cheek. The divine infant places his hand on her chin and clutches her blue veil. She supports his back and bottom with her own hands in a loving embrace This display of affection becomes all the more poignant when one thinks of the Child's destiny and how the Blessed Mother will once again hold her son's broken and dead body in a Pietà.

But here, for now, time and space are erased in a gilt background of serene repose and happiness. The compassion and tenderness that underscore the Eleousa icons become resplendent here. The stars on the Mary's shoulders and brow are ancient symbols of virginity. This is the Theotokos, the Christ-bearer, the Mother of God, portrayed in a most natural and loving way. Perhaps this is the loving quality that struck Bernadette when she first saw the image. Was hers an emotional response to a profoundly intellectual idea? Just as Mary revealed herself to the peasant girl in her native dialect, saying to her, "I am the Immaculate Conception," Bernadette had no notion of what these words even meant. She had to ask her parish priest for an explanation, and her naiveté bolstered the veracity of her vision. Hardened skeptics like Émile Zola would rail against the phenomenon of Lourdes, and yet the crowds grew in number year after year, making the shrine the greatest pilgrimage spot in all of human history.

Bernadette wanted a duplicate of the icon placed in the grotto, but a statue of the Virgin was placed there instead. Mary told Bernadette that she could not promise her happiness in this life, only in the life to come. But this story of the image of the Virgin does have a happy ending. On the day of the last apparition, on the 16th of July 1858, Bernadette was not able to be at the grotto because the police had barricaded it. So Bernadette went to the other side of the River Gave, where the Virgin appeared to her in spite of the barriers. Almost on the exact spot where Bernadette prayed in that last vision, a modern church dedicated to Saint Bernadette was consecrated in 1988. It is there that the French conference of bishops meets every fall. And it is there, in the sanctuary of the church, that a replica icon of Our Lady of Cambrai was placed, an image that Bernadette claimed was the truest image of the loving woman she beheld in rapture.

THE VIRGIN OF GUADALUPE

The Virgin of Guadalupe (1531), painting on fabric, 67 x 41.3 in., The Shrine of Our Lady of Guadalupe, Mexico City, Mexico

Great art has contributed to the culture of the Church. But once in a rare while another kind of sacred image appears that does not seem to be the work of human hands. The Shroud of Turin and the Veil of Veronica are examples. But in the western hemisphere the greatest and most potent image attributed to heavenly intervention is that of Our Lady of Guadalupe.

It appeared in 1531 on the cactus fiber cloak, or *tilma*, of a native who had been baptized and given the name Juan Diego. It had been ten years since Hernando Cortés had overtaken the Aztec Empire and subjugated the land that he called New Spain. With great difficulty the missionaries tried to make converts among the native peoples. Juan Diego's conversion had been sincere, and he was on his way to Mass one cold December morning when our Lady appeared to him on a hill called Tepeyac and spoke to him in his native tongue. She ordered him to tell Bishop Juan Zumárraga of Mexico City to build a church there in her honor. When he finally gained an audience with Bishop Zumárraga, the good bishop hesitated, not knowing whether to believe the native's astonishing story. He asked Juan Diego to have the Lady give him a sign in order to assist him in his decision. On his return home, Juan Diego again encountered the Virgin, who bid him to return to the bishop with the same message the next day. She would provide him with a sign. Upon returning to his village, however, Juan learned that his beloved uncle was near death, and he urgently bid him to find a priest to assist him in his final hours.

Now burdened with two urgent requests, Juan Diego opted to aid his uncle first, by finding a priest. He purposefully took another route around Tepeyac in order to avoid the Virgin. But she intercepted him, assuring him that his uncle would be cured. She ordered him to climb the barren hill and gather the flowers he would find on its summit and take them to the bishop, who had requested a sign. Juan Diego did so, and before departing on his journey the Virgin herself arranged the miraculous blooms in the folds of his cloak. This time Juan Diego encountered even more difficulty in gaining admittance to the bishop, but he persisted, and when he was finally ushered in and opened up his tilma to the cascade of unseasonable flowers, he was surprised to watch the prelate fall to his knees. The flowers alone were not what had astonished the bishop. Juan Diego soon discovered that our Lady had provided an even more marvelous sign. It was a portrait of her as he had seen her, an image that has become the most powerful and beloved likeness of the Virgin in all of human history.

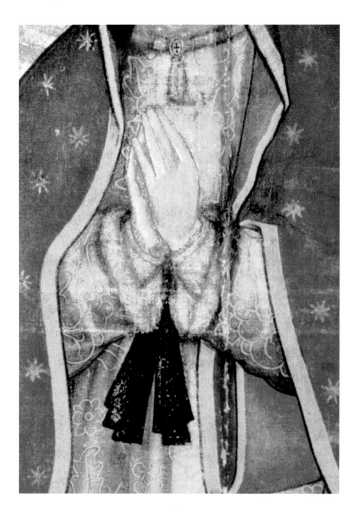

She had dark skin and hair, like the native peoples, who were soon attracted to her image and persuaded by what they saw. Though she would seem to be a goddess, wearing a cloak of stars and blocking the sun's rays while standing on the moon, held aloft by an attendant angel, her head was bowed in humility. Something greater was coming through her. Beneath her folded hands a maternity sash was tied. She was pregnant. A new beginning was about to unfold.

A shrine was immediately built on Tepeyac, where Juan Diego spent the rest of his days as caretaker and guardian of the indelible portrait. The power of that image soon became evident. In the next decade, between eight and ten million natives were converted to the Faith. Not since apostolic times had so many conversions taken place. The vast number more than made up for the losses suffered in a Europe that was now divided by the Reformation.

When asked under what name the Virgin had appeared to him, Juan Diego responded with a phrase that seemed to the Spanish chronicler's ear to sound like "Guadalupe," the site of a venerated cult of the Virgin back in his native country. But scholars believe that Juan Diego was actually saying in his native Aztec dialect the word *coatlallope*, which phonetically sounds like Guadalupe but actually means "one who treads upon the serpent." Since the serpent god had been the very foundation of the Aztec religion that demanded human sacrifice atop stone pyramids erected in his honor, our Lady's description of herself in his native tongue had a more profound meaning. It was she who would overcome the serpent by bringing forth the one true God, whose own sacrifice would take place in the ritual of the Mass celebrated in churches built atop the ruins of the pagan temples. (Coincidentally, it has been noted that the folds of garment around her right foot resemble that of a serpent's head with its tongue sticking out.) The dual meaning of the word Guadalupe in effect united two peoples, the Spaniard and the native, forging a new culture whose identity is forever marked by this miraculous image.

The tilma should have disintegrated long ago, but it remains intact. Centuries of veneration, of touching, of kissing, of candle smoke and incense have not dulled its color. It has survived the ravages of flood, plague, fire, and even an exploding bomb planted underneath it by agents of an anticlerical and Masonic government. It has been the source of numerous miracles, the cause of much healing, and a consolation to multitudes. Up to twenty million pilgrims visit the shrine every year, making it the most popular religious pilgrimage site in the western hemisphere. Painted copies of it have been reverently produced over the centuries. New versions were customarily touched to the original, in order to transmit its miraculous properties.

When one such copy was presented to Pope Benedict XIV in 1754, he wept and uttered words derived from Psalm 147 that underscore the divine gift that has become the glory of Mexico: *He has not dealt in like manner with any other nation.*

In 1945 Pope Pius XII declared that the Virgin of Guadalupe was the Queen of Mexico and the Empress of the Americas.

Thus a mysterious and mystical icon reflects best the majesty of Mary who is Queen of both heaven and earth. She cares for her children as they journey through this vale of tears and struggle to rise above the temptations and sorrows of this life to join her Son in the everlasting bliss of the life to come.

The words she spoke to reassure Juan Diego can thus be applied to everyone:

"Do not be distressed…. Am I not here with you who am your Mother?

"Are you not under my shadow and protection? Do not grieve or be disturbed by anything."

ART CREDITS

Page 95: Cristóbal de Villalpando (c. 1649–1714), *La Dolorosa*, National Museum del Virreinato, Tepotzotlán, Mexico. © Rights reserved.

Page 98: Rogier van der Weyden (c. 1399–1464), *Christ Appearing to His Mother* (1442–45), Gemäldegalerie, Berlin, Germany. © BPK, Berlin, Dist. RMN-GP | Jörg P. Anders.

Page 102: Maurice Denis (1870–1943), *Pentecost* (1934), Apse of the Church of the Holy Spirit, Paris, France. © SuperStock/Leemage.

Page 105: Rogier van der Weyden (c. 1399–1464) (after), *Saint Luke Drawing a Portrait of the Virgin* (c. 1435–40), Groeningemuseum, Bruges, Belgium. © Lukas - Art in Flanders VZW | Bridgeman Images.

Page 108: Titian (1490–1576), *The Assumption* (1516–18), Church of Santa Maria Gloriosa dei Frari, Venice, Italy. © Luisa Ricciarini | Leemage.

Page 111: Hans Memling (c. 1433–1494), *Saint John on Patmos Gazing at a Vision of the Apocalypse* (1474–79), Memling Museum, Saint John's Hospital, Bruges, Belgium. © Bridgeman | Lukas - Art in Flanders VZW.

Page 115: Anonymous, *The Crowning of Mary* (late 20th c.), Private Collection, Ocumicho, Mexico. © Christopher Silva.

Page 118: Albretch Dürer (1471–1528), *The Feast of the Rose Garlands* (1506), Narodni Gallery, Prague, Czech Republic. © FineArtimages | Leemage.

Page 122: Attributed to the Netherlandish painter Goswijn van der Weyden (1455–1543), *The Fifteen Mysteries and the Virgin of the Rosary* (1515–20), Metropolitan Museum of Art, New York, USA. © The MMA, dist. RMN-GP | image of the MMA.

Page 125: Hans von Kulmbach (1480–1528), *The Heavenly Rosary* (c. 1510), Thyssen-Bornemisza Museum, Madrid, Spain. © Electa | Leemage.

Page 128: Fra Bartolomeo (1472–1517), *The Vision of Saint Bernard* (1504), Uffizi Gallery, Florence, Italy. © Luisa Ricciarini | Leemage.

Page 132: Francisco de Zurbarán (1598–1664), *Mater Misericordiæ Sheltering the Carthusians* (c. 1655), Museum of Fine Arts, Seville, Spain. © Aisa | Leemage.

Page 136: Giambattista Tiepolo (1696–1770), *The Madonna of Mount Carmel* (1721–27), Pinacoteca di Brera, Milan, Italy. © Luisa Ricciarini | Leemage.

Page 141: Raphael (1483–1520), *The Madonna Standing on Clouds with Saint Sixtus and Barbara* (aka the *Sistine Madonna*) (1512–13), Gëmaldegalerie Alte Meister, Dresden, Germany. © FineArtimages | Leemage.

Page 145: Paolo Veronese (1528–1588), *Allegory of the Battle of Lepanto* (c. 1572), Gallerie dell'Academia, Venice, Italy. © Luisa Ricciarini | Leemage.

Page 148: Anonymous Italian, *Icon of Our Lady of Cambrai* (c. 1340), Church of Notre-Dame de Grace, Cambrai, France. © Studio Déclic, Cambrai. Photo : Vincent Bertin.

Page 151: *The Virgin of Guadalupe* (1531), The Shrine of Our Lady of Guadalupe, Mexico City, Mexico. © All Rights reserved.